AUSTRALIA *The Greatest Island*

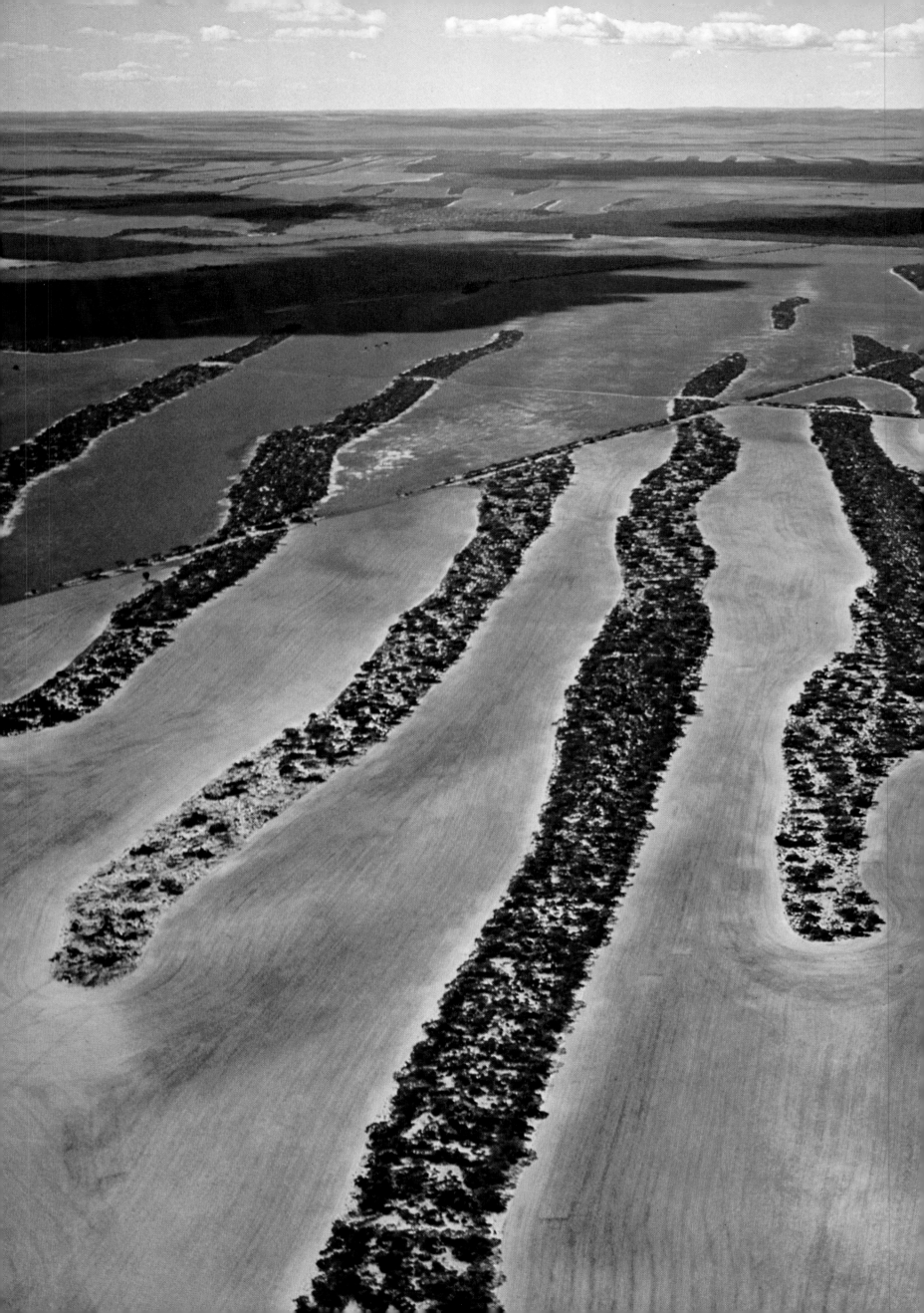

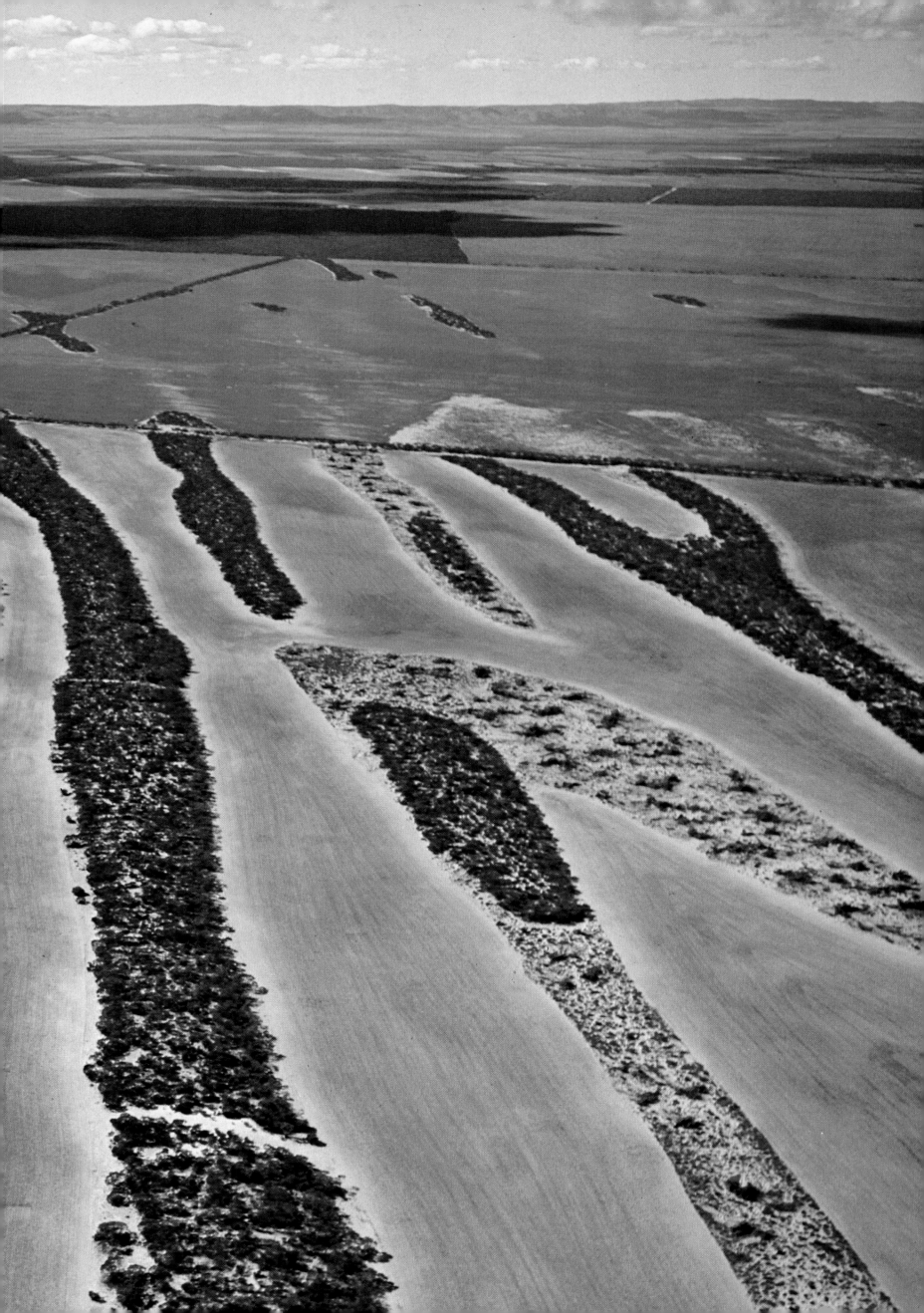

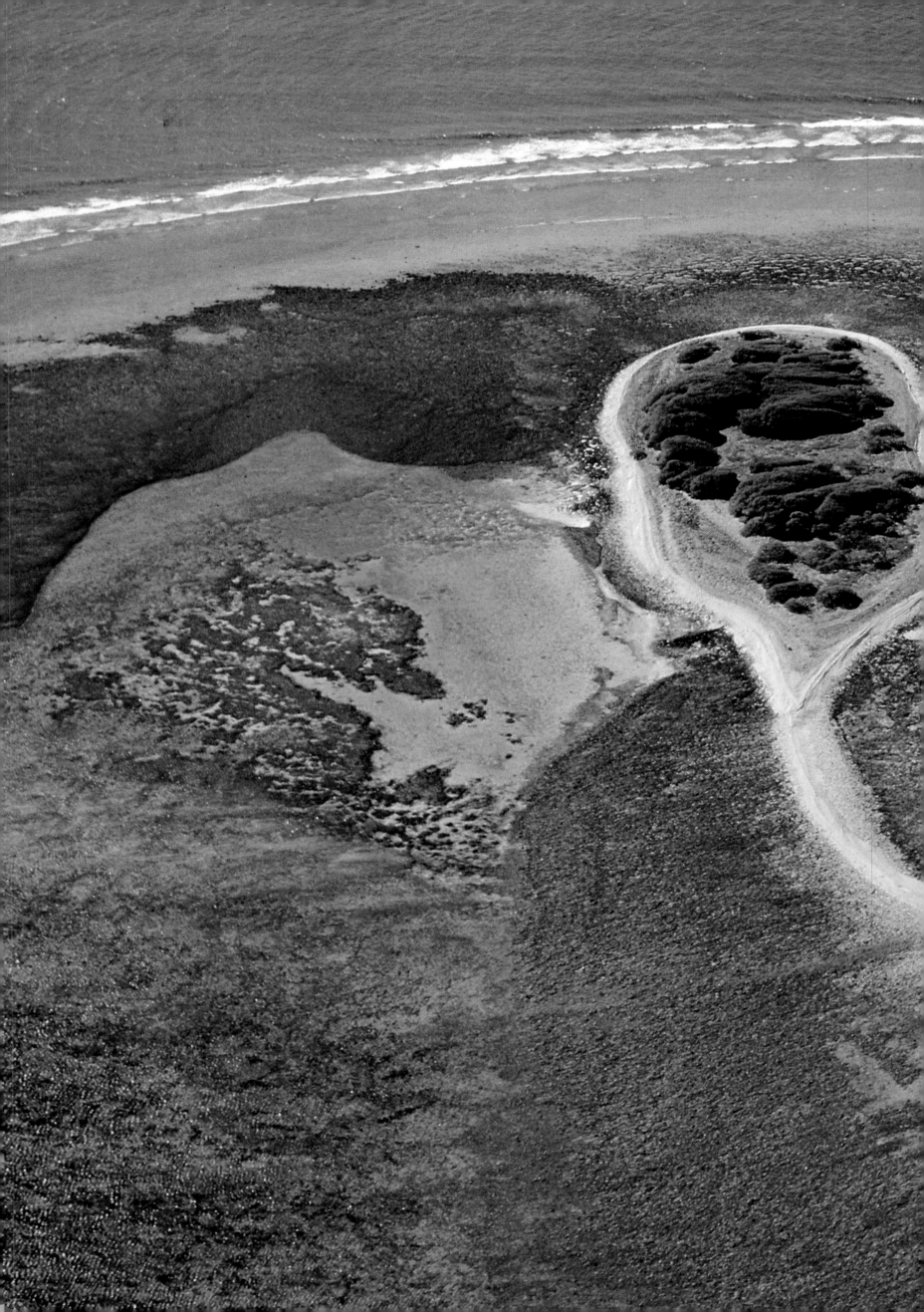

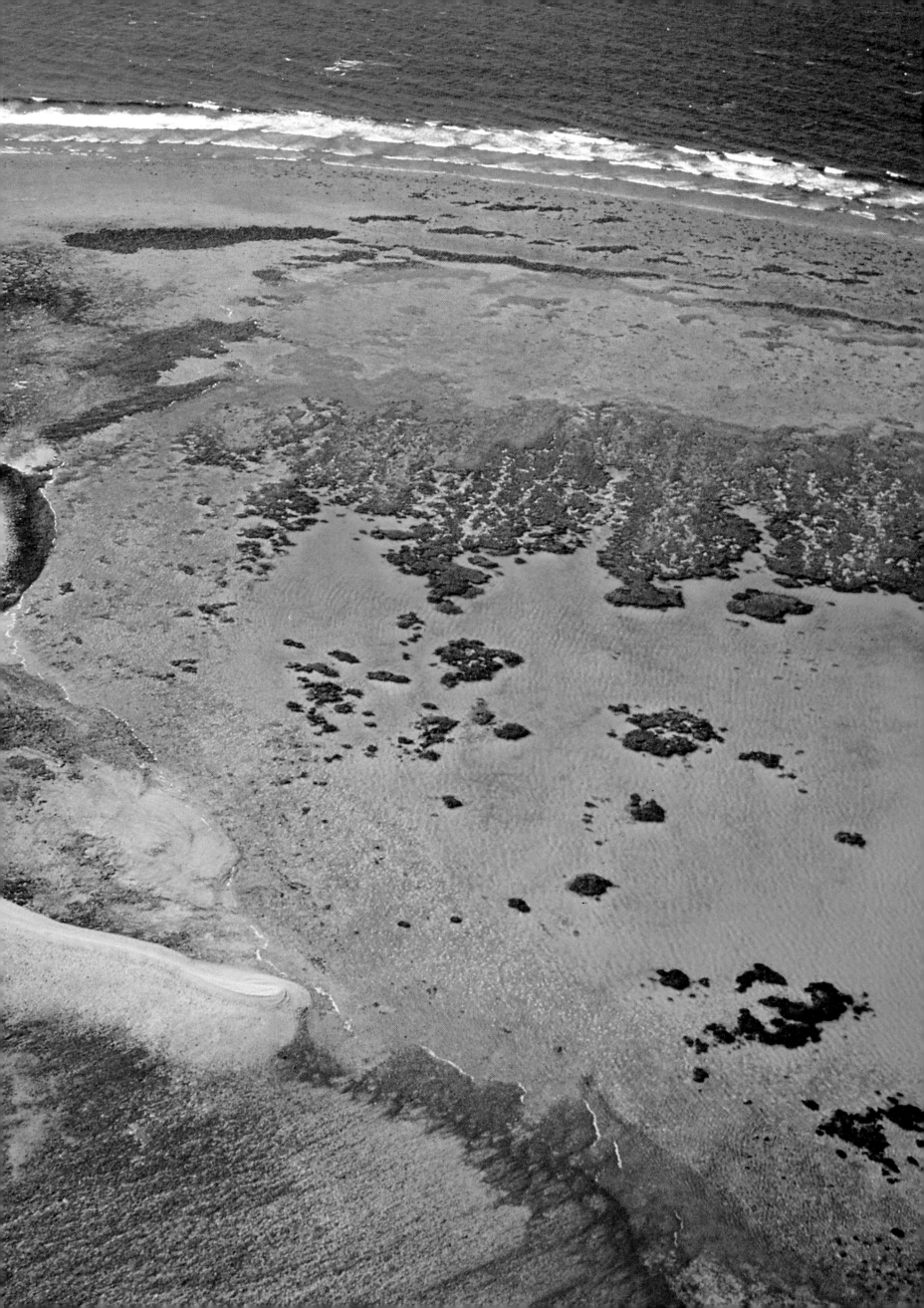

**AN AERIAL EXPLORATION OF
THE AUSTRALIAN COASTLINE**

AUSTRALIA *The Greatest Island*

Text by
ROBERT RAYMOND

Photography by
REG MORRISON

LANSDOWNE

PRECEDING PAGES:

PAGES 2-3: Colourful eroded sandstone formations of Port Campbell National Park, Victoria. The carving of these formations is the result of wave action by the seas, which are steadily eating through the coast, once an ancient sea floor but now raised high above sea level.

PAGES 4-5: Farming patterns on the landscape of Eyre Peninsula, South Australia. The dark parallel strips of low, vegetated sand dunes are separated by ploughed land. The dunes in the background lie like islands in a green sea of winter wheat.

PAGES 6-7: Hoskyn Island, in the Bunker Group off southern Queensland. This typical coral "tadpole" has been formed on a low platform reef, from sand and rubble heaped up by the prevailing wind and waves. At high tide the sea may cover the fringing reef and the lagoon, leaving only the island and its sandy tail exposed.

PAGES 8-9: Salt patterns at Lake McLeod, Western Australia. Natural tidal flats with salt-encrusted islands (foreground) contrast with the man-made evaporation ponds of a commercial salt works. The salt industry made the first large-scale use of solar energy in Australia.

PAGES 10-11: Ribbon Reef, near Lizard Island, north Queensland. This area is part of the true Outer Barrier reef, which runs along the edge of the continental shelf and creates a vast lagoon off the Queensland coast. The breaks in the Outer Barrier are deep channels. It was through such a passage that Captain Cook escaped to the open sea in 1770, after his voyage along the eastern coastline.

ACKNOWLEDGEMENTS:

The photographic material for this book, and for the television series *Pelican's Progress,* was compiled during an aerial expedition jointly sponsored by The Rigby Group Australia and the Seven National Network.

Photographs for the book were taken by international award-winning photographer Reg Morrison, using Hasselblad and Nikon cameras and Kodak Ektachrome film. The text was written by Robert Raymond, who also produced the television series.

The flight commander for the expedition was Vic Walton, a Flying Officer in the Royal Australian Air Force Reserve, and a test and demonstration pilot for the Government Aircraft Factory, Melbourne. Mr Walton's charter and survey floatplane company, Aquatic Airways, Sydney, provided the three Cessna aircraft used on the expedition. Other pilots were John Smith, an experienced ferry pilot with Navair, Sydney; Ian Chessel, who has extensive floatplane experience in New Guinea and Queensland's "gulf" country; and John Seaton, a former Qantas captain. Flight engineer on the expedition was Greg Booth, of Icarus Aviation, Sydney.

A great deal of the success of this expedition is due to the helpful and understanding co-operation of air traffic controllers and other personnel of the Department of Transport in all parts of Australia.

Distributed by Gary Allen Pty Ltd
9 Cooper Street, Smithfield NSW 2164

Published by Lansdowne Publishing Pty Ltd
Level 5, 70 George Street, Sydney NSW 2000, Australia

First Published by Ure Smith 1979
Reprinted by Lansdowne Press 1980 (twice), 1981, 1982, 1984, 1986, 1987,
Reprinted by Lansdowne Publishing Pty Ltd 1994

© Copyright Lansdowne Publishing Pty Ltd
© Copyright heading typography: Bruno Grasswill 1981

Produced in Australia by the Publisher
Typeset in Australia by Savage Type, Brisbane
Printed in Singapore by Toppan Printing Co. (Pte) Ltd

National Library of Australia Cataloguing-in-Publication Data
  Raymond, Robert. 1922-
  Australia, the greatest island.
  ISBN 1 86302 400 X.
  1. Shorelines - Australia - Pictorial works. 2. Coasts - Australia
  - Pictorial works. I. Morrison, Reg. II. Title.
  919.4

Preface

When Matthew Flinders set out in 1801 on the first circumnavigation of the Australian continent, only a few sections of the coastline had been properly charted. It was his commission to fill in the blanks on the map. Flinders did remarkably well, but in many places the waters were so treacherous that his ship, the *Investigator,* was unable to follow the coastline closely. Then off Arnhem Land, with the task barely half completed, the *Investigator* became unseaworthy. Flinders had to stand far out to sea, making a precarious run round the western and southern coasts to Sydney.

Today, nearly two centuries later, vast stretches of the Australian coastline remain, because of their remoteness and their inaccessibility, virtually as unknown as when Flinders sailed past them. It was to fill in some of the gaps in awareness of such areas that we set out in 1978 on the first photographic circumnavigation of the entire continent of Australia, including Tasmania.

Following in the wake of Matthew Flinders, we started from Cape Leeuwin in the south-west corner and travelled in an anti-clockwise direction around the entire coastline. But where Flinders was often forced far out from the coast, and in many places could only guess what lay beyond the cliffs or line of surf, we flew at low altitude along the shoreline in seaplanes. We chose these aircraft with floats because of the freedom they gave us to land at will on estuaries, bays, rivers, and lakes, enabling us to explore the remotest regions of Australia.

Our overwhelming impression of this great island-continent is of the diversity and wild beauty of the coastline. It is often desolate, and sometimes harsh, but magnificent in the way it has retained the unaltered, unpolluted serenity of the natural environment — a pristine quality that is becoming increasingly rare elsewhere in the world.

And yet, at intervals in our seven-week expedition, we were also stimulated to come upon the scattered fingerprints of man around the enormous pie-crust of the continent — the cities, harbours, farmlands, mines, holiday resorts and mission settlements dotted along the endless coastline.

For Australians, many of whom live in communities still isolated by immense distances, and for those in other parts of the world who may still wonder about *Terra australis incognita,* the "Unknown South Land", we hope this book will help to fill in some gaps in our knowledge of this island-continent — and perhaps even link us all a little more closely by tracing out the one and only frontier we have, where the land meets the encircling sea from which it once emerged.

ROBERT RAYMOND
REG MORRISON

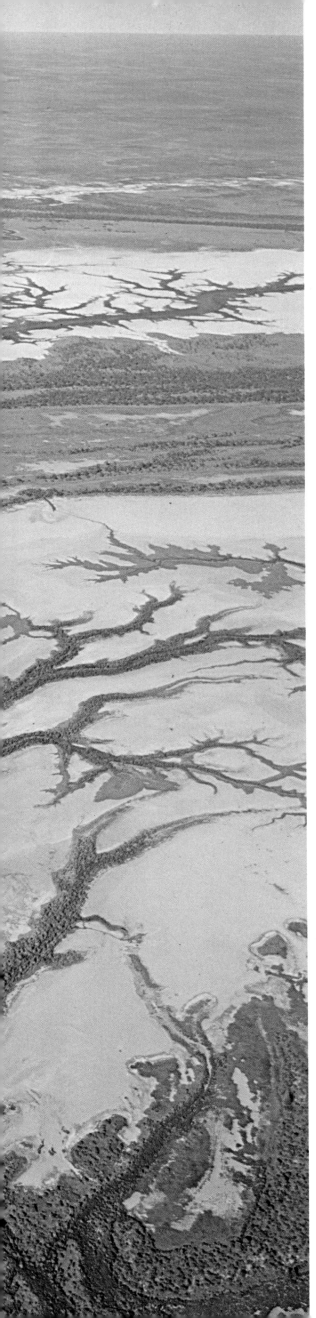

Contents

LEFT: Drainage patterns near the
Staaten River, north of Karumba,
Queensland. The tree-like channels are
created by the rapid outflow of the
tide, which cuts down through the salt
crust to expose the underlying mud
and sand.

Introduction

Australia is an island — the greatest island of all. Extending from within a few degrees of the Equator to the edge of the Antarctic region, its surface covers an area of approximately 7,700,000 square kilometres. Its immense coastline measures some 36,700 kilometres — nearly the circumference of the earth — and is washed by three oceans, the Pacific, Southern and Indian, and four seas, the Tasman, Coral, Arafura and Timor.

This book is a visual celebration of Australia's coastline; for it is the coastline that gives an island its identity, its outline on the map. Where Australia is concerned, it is an identity of breathtaking unexpectedness. For although the interior of the continent is notable for its lack of relief, and often seems flat and featureless, the coastline is full of surprises. Rocky headlands enclose hidden, snow-white beaches; mangrove-lined estuaries wind between shimmering coastal dunes; towering cliffs alternate with undulating green heathlands; islands of every size and shape lie off the shore, interspersed with countless coral reefs.

The coastline is a valuable guide to an island's history because it provides a geological record of past events. As the earth heaves and sinks, the levels of the oceans rise and fall, and through this process the coastline is slowly but continually being shaped and re-shaped. Australia's bays and inlets, drowned river valleys and wave-cut platforms at the foot of cliffs show that the continent is remarkably old and stable.

Australia has been separated from the other large landmasses for at least 45 million years. Before this, according to the now-accepted theory of continental drift, it formed part of a vast "supercontinent" in the south, called Gondwanaland. The other landmasses making up Gondwanaland were Antarctica, Africa, South America and India. About 150 million years ago this "supercontinent" began to break up, with the continents beginning a slow drift to their present positions. Australia and Antarctica were the last to separate, with Australia setting off on a course which in another 50 million years is expected to take it near the coast of China.

How this happens is explained by the theory of plate tectonics. The ocean floors and landmasses of the earth ride on rigid plates of light rock, 70-150 kilometres thick, which slide across the earth's mantle, the "plastic" under-layer of the earth's crust. These plates may move as much as 10 centimetres a year. The Indo-Australian plate on which Australia rides is very large, and the continent is located in its centre, far from the turbulent margins where the plates jostle past one another. This explains why Australia has experienced very few convulsions or upheavals in comparison with other continents.

The last significant upheaval was the so-called "Kosciusko Uplift", which ended some 2 million years ago. This resulted in the series of almost continuous uplands of the Great Divide, or Great Dividing Range, which extends from the Grampian Range in the south to Cape York Peninsula in the north. During this disturbance some sections of the coastline were submerged, producing the magnificent cliffs and rock formations of south-west Tasmania.

A later and more gentle change in the coastline was the slow but long-continued subsidence of the continental shelf along the Queensland coast, which resulted in the growth of the Great Barrier Reef system. Extending for 2000 kilometres, this system contains thousands of platform reefs and coral islands which have developed in the warm, sheltered lagoon between the Outer Barrier and the coast.

The coastline has played an important role throughout the history of human occupation of this island-continent. In the past, because of variations in sea level, Australia has at times been joined by dry land to New Guinea and Tasmania. Such situations must clearly have helped the original entry into and settlement of the continent by Aboriginals from Asia, more than 50,000 years ago. But when the seas rose Australia became isolated, and its vast distances and arid centre did not encourage easy settlement. For this reason, from the time the first settlers arrived, right through the subsequent European discovery and colonisation, the bulk of the population has always lived along the fertile rim on the continent.

Today most of the major centres of population, including the State capital cities, are located on the coast. Seventy per cent of the population live on the eastern shores, and the remainder occupy scattered towns and cities around the rest of the continent. And yet, because of the enormous length of the coastline, there are vast stretches between the inhabited areas which are sparsely populated or even completely deserted. These areas are by-passed by regular air, sea and overland communications, and because they are rarely visited they remain a mystery to the majority of Australians.

The coastline runs like a silver thread through the recorded history of Australia. It appears first in tentative sketches of haphazard landfalls made by navigators heading for other destinations. It is shown with increasing clarity in the meticulous charts and records kept by such men as Captain James Cook and Matthew Flinders, who painstakingly traced the shores and gave the shadowy continent its shape on the map. It appears here, for the first time, in all its diversity, in the panoramic aerial photographs which capture the natural and man-made patterns that make up the Australian coast.

Cape Leeuwin to Eyre Peninsula

The great southern coastline, stretching from the south-west corner of Western Australia across the Great Australian Bight to Eyre Peninsula in South Australia, is one of the wildest and most untouched frontiers of the Australian continent. It begins at Cape Leeuwin, on the stormy, wave-washed south-west corner. Dutch navigators, outward bound around the Cape of Good Hope, first sighted this part of the coast early in the seventeenth century when they were pushed south during their journeys to the colonies in the East Indies.

To the east, past Albany and Esperance, the coastline arches upwards into the vast sweep of the Great Australian Bight, one of the most astonishing features of this or any other continent. Nowhere else in the world has the land thrown up such mighty ramparts to the sea as the wall of cliffs that extends along the edge of the Bight. Rising from the seas crashing at their base, the cliffs run from horizon to horizon, unbroken by inlet, estuary or gap; behind them the flat Nullarbor Plain recedes into the haze. Near the head of the Bight the cliffs vanish as suddenly as they began, and the character of the coastline changes. Beetling walls of rock give way to wide, gentle beaches and undulating sand dunes that continue almost to the tip of Eyre Peninsula.

But in all this tremendous stretch of coastline there is only a handful of towns and settlements. It remains virtually as desolate and unpeopled as it was in 1627, when Pieter Nuijts in the *Gulden Zeepaert* (Golden Seahorse) made the first crossing of the Bight.

LEFT: The unbroken, seemingly endless wall of the Nullarbor cliffs extends to a misty horizon. The seas, continually undercutting the limestone ramparts, have brought down the heaps of rocks at the base of the cliffs. The Eyre Highway, linking South Australia with Western Australia, in places runs close to the cliff edge.

LEFT AND ABOVE: Cape Leeuwin, Australia's south-western tip. The blunt bow of the continent, it is forever butting the great swells that roll up from the Southern Ocean, driven by the ceaseless winds of the "roaring forties". The Cape is named after the Dutch ship *Leeuwin* which is thought to have sighted this part of the coast in 1622 while heading for Batavia. Today it is a national park, and the only permanent inhabitants are the families of the lighthouse keepers. The Leeuwin light is a welcome sight for ships seeking a landfall after the long run east across the Indian Ocean. To the east of the Cape is the beginning of Flinders Bay, so named because Matthew Flinders sheltered there in 1801 before setting out in the *Investigator* on what was to become his historic circumnavigation of the continent.

OVERLEAF: The south coast near Point d'Entrecasteaux. The long frontal dunes, heaped up behind the wide beach by the prevailing seas, are being colonised and stabilised by tenacious shrubs. The older dunes behind are slashed by blowouts, grooves cut through the vegetation and sand by the south-westerly gales.

21

LEFT: The smooth contoured walls of Chatham Island, polished by the incessant pounding of the waves.
ABOVE: The rugged outcrop of Chatham Island and its outlying rocks shows the ancient granite that makes up the south-west corner of Australia's coast. Over millions of years the seas have worn down the surrounding rock of the island, leaving a harder inner core standing isolated from the mainland.

LEFT: The coastline east of Albany, in the south-west corner of Australia. Rain-laden westerly winds continually blow across this part of the coast, making it one of the wettest parts of the continent. The softly rounded granite hills (foreground) gradually merge with the Whoogarup Range.
TOP: East of the Whoogarup Range the coastline rolls out into a broad plain, relieved by drifting dunes which spill like cream across the landscape.
ABOVE: A family of brumbies gallops over flowering heathland in the Whoogarup Range.

ABOVE: Islands of the Archipelago of the Recherche. This group of islands, numbering almost one hundred, extends nearly 200 kilometres eastwards along the coast from Esperance Bay. The archipelago was named after *La Recherche,* the flagship of French Rear-Admiral Joseph Bruni d'Entrecasteaux who visited the islands in 1792. (Esperance was named after his support ship, *L'Esperance,* meaning "hope".) The islands vary in size and shape, but all are made of granite. They are uninhabited, and many have never been visited because of the difficulty of landing on their rocky, wave-washed shores.

RIGHT: Hair seals, near Esperance. These seals, valued for their oil, were almost wiped out by hunters in the nineteenth century. Today they are a protected species and their numbers are steadily increasing.

FAR RIGHT: Woody Island, in the Archipelago of the Recherche. This large island lies close to Esperance, and is one of the few in the group that can be visited. A landing stage has been built by an Esperance tug-boat operator who runs day trips from the mainland when sea conditions permit.

RIGHT: Sand dunes near Point Culver. The explorer Edward John Eyre stumbled across these dunes in 1841, nearly dead from thirst during his famous first crossing of the desert fringing the Great Australian Bight. His sole companion, an Aborigine, showed him how to dig down into the hollows between the dunes to find water.

ABOVE TOP: Ruins at Eucla, Western Australia. A tiny settlement was established here in 1885 as a relay station on the east-west telegraph line. It was abandoned in 1927 when the coastal line was closed down.

ABOVE: A baby whale and its mother shelter in the shallow waters of Israelite Bay, at the western extremity of the Great Australian Bight.

ABOVE: An angular bend breaks the monotony on this long stretch of Old Eyre Highway, near Koonalda. This road, now by-passed, was a dusty, spring-breaking track that made the crossing of the Nullarbor Plain a fairly hazardous expedition.

ABOVE LEFT: Cliffs at the edge of the Nullarbor Plain, on the Great Australian Bight.

LEFT: Coastal dunes near Eucla. Driven by onshore winds, the sand is steadily moving inland.

RIGHT: The entrance to Koonalda Cave, on the Nullarbor Plain, South Australia. The wide opening, nearly 100 metres across, was created by the collapse of a cavern near the surface. The cave itself lies deeper underground and measures up to 122 metres wide and 76 metres high. Including its system of tunnels, which branch out from the main cavern, it extends for more than 300 metres. As can be seen from the tracks, there has been much traffic to and from Koonalda: Aborigines used the cave as a flint quarry more than 20 thousand years ago; in more recent times the local station owner has pumped water from the cave for his stock; and since 1957 anthropologists and archaeologists have visited the cave to excavate its floor and study the mysterious wall markings.

ABOVE: A collapsed cave on the Nullarbor Plain. Rainwater percolating through the great depth of porous limestone which makes up the Plain has in many places dissolved and hollowed out large underground caverns. When the roof of such a cave becomes too thin it collapses, as this one has done.

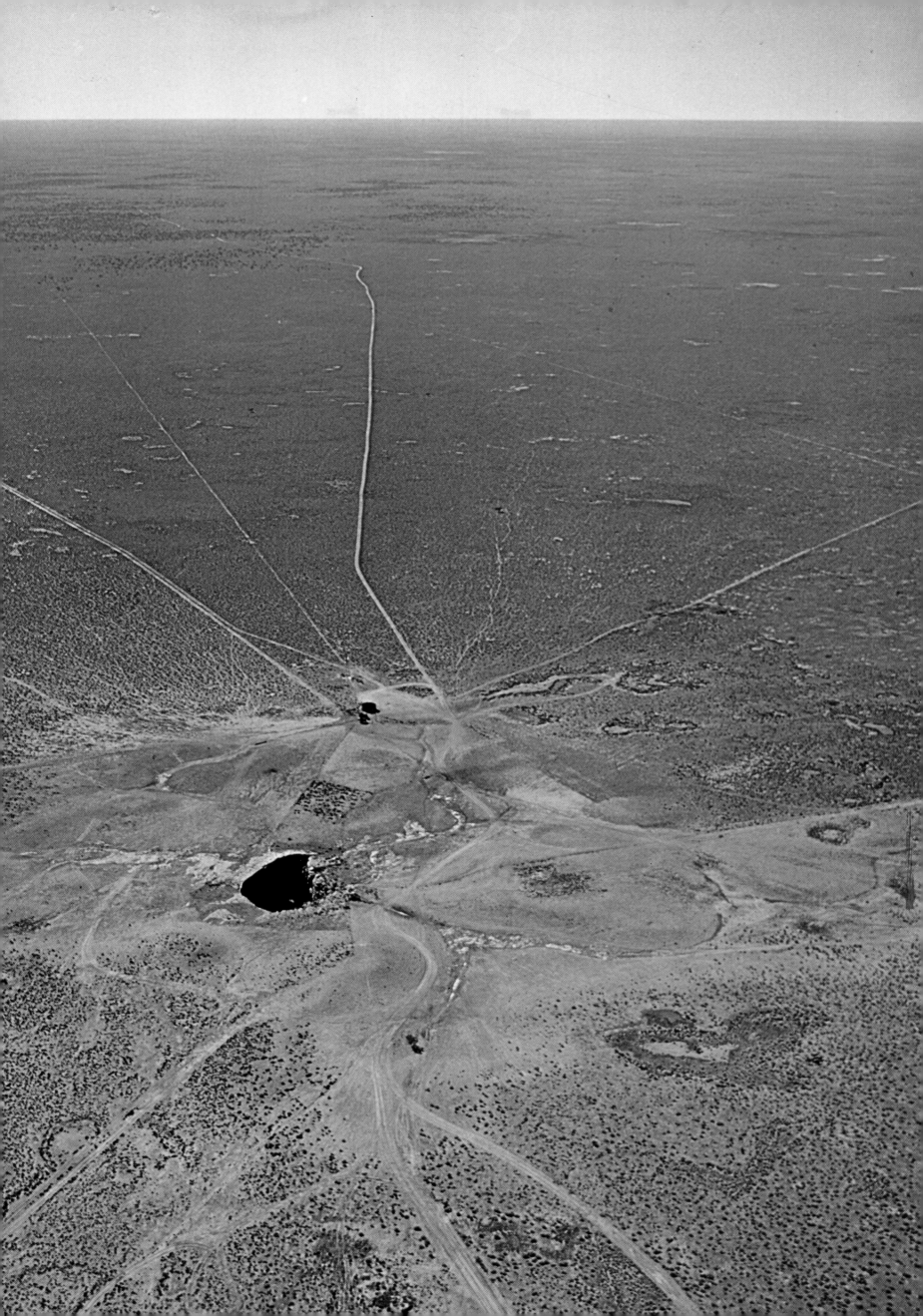

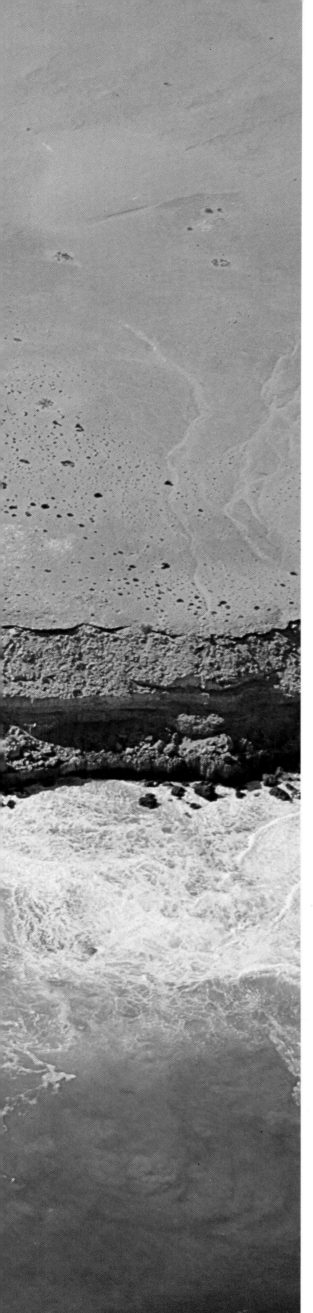

LEFT: Cape Nuyts, South Australia.
This cape was named by Matthew
Flinders in 1802, in honour of
Pieter Nuijts, master of the Dutch
Gulden Zeepaert (Golden Seahorse),
the first European ship to venture into
the Great Australian Bight. Nuijts
sailed about as far east as this in 1627
before turning back.
ABOVE: On the calm waters of Fowlers
Bay, near Ceduna, a fisherman heads
for his weekend fishing ground.

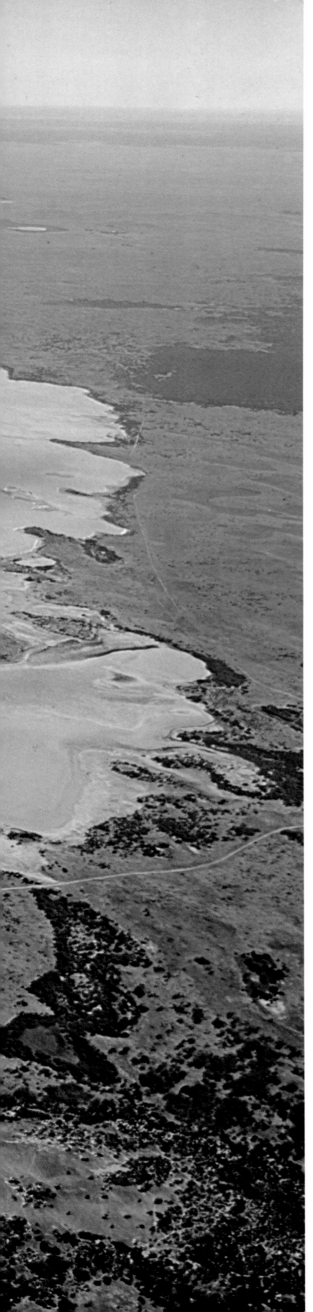

LEFT: Lake Hamilton, South Australia, one of several salt lakes on the west coast of Eyre Peninsula. These lakes are produced by a high rate of evaporation acting on shallow freshwater lagoons, which form where the run-off from the low-lying hinterland is not sufficiently strong to break through the coastal dunes to the sea or where former outlets have been closed by growing dunes. The picture clearly shows the gradation of salination, from the deep, slightly brackish water at the top, to the saltier shallows in the centre, and finally to the intensely salty pools of brine in the foreground.

ABOVE: Cliffs near Cape Blanche, on the Eyre Peninsula. This area consists of very ancient sedimentary rocks which have lain undisturbed for hundreds of millions of years, their strata as evenly bedded as when they were laid down. Where the seas have worn into the sediments, the result is this strikingly scalloped shoreline.

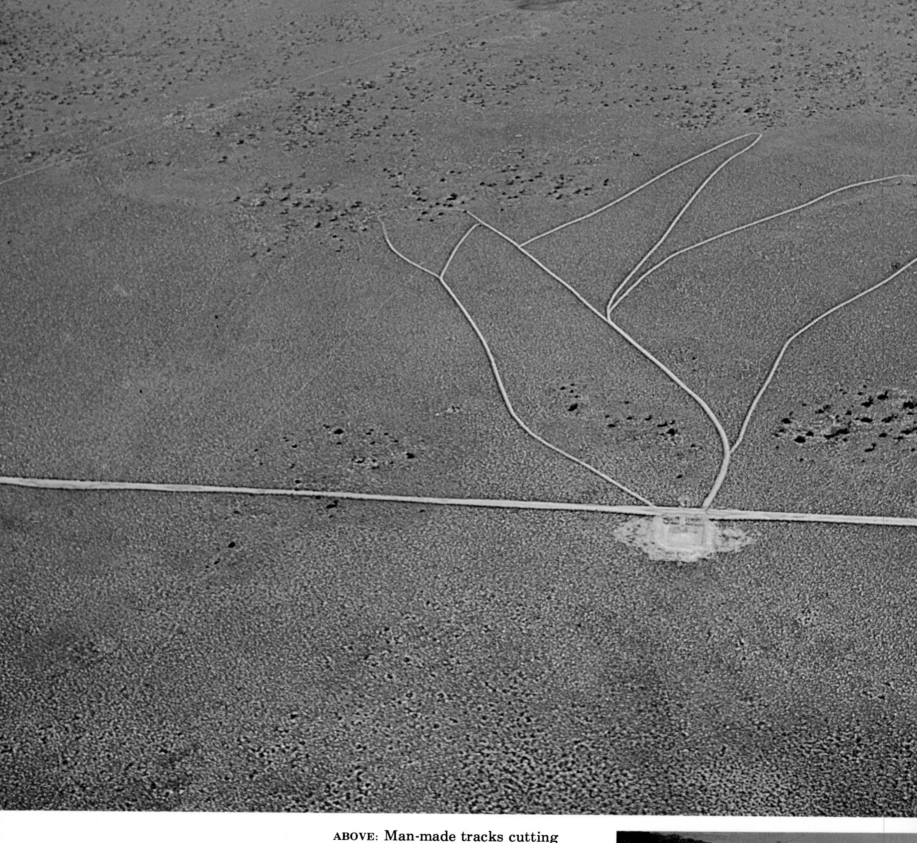

ABOVE: Man-made tracks cutting through the grasslands decorate this broad natural carpet near Cowell, on the eastern side of Eyre Peninsula.
RIGHT: Farming patterns near Cowell. Rivers of green winter wheat flow between dark parallel banks of vegetated sand dunes.
FAR RIGHT: The patterns are reversed: these green patches, also near Cowell, are islands of rocky ground in a sea of ploughed land.

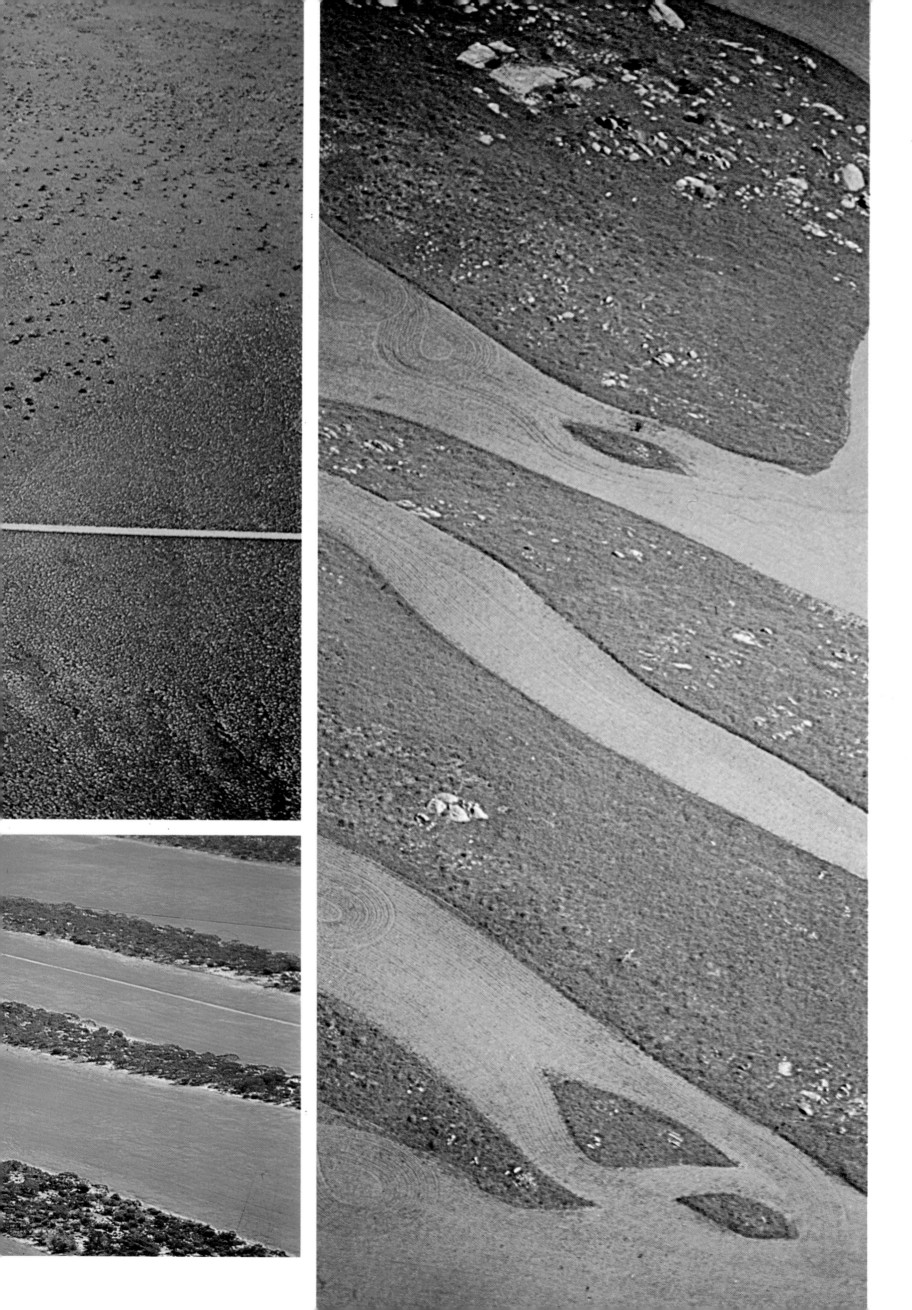

Yorke Peninsula to Wilson's Promontory

The coastline from Yorke Peninsula in South Australia, across the Victorian border to Cape Otway at the entrance to Bass Strait, has an ancient, worn-down appearance, as if little has changed for millions of years. This is in fact true; parts of the coastline have hardly altered since Permian times, 230 million years ago.

Two major breaks in the low coastline are Spencer Gulf and Gulf St Vincent, which cut deeply into the underside of the continent. They are all that remains of a vast sea trough that crossed the centre of Australia and linked up with the Gulf of Carpentaria, more than 70 million years ago. The two gulfs are rift valleys that were flooded by the great rise in sea level at the end of the last Ice Age.

East of Gulf St Vincent lies the rocky spine of South Australia — the Flinders Ranges–Mount Lofty mountain chain. This ridge runs northwards from the coast into the arid interior, and also extends south-west across the coast to form the core of Kangaroo Island, which is cut off from the mainland by a narrow passage.

From Kangaroo Island the coast sweeps away to the south-east, with little physical relief. Even the continent's greatest river, the Murray, enters the sea not through an impressive estuary but unobtrusively, across a shallow sandbar lying between an otherwise unbroken stretch of coastal dunes.

Where South Australia joins Victoria, however, the cones of extinct volcanoes, some of which were active less than five thousand years ago, stand out boldly on the flat landscape. The city of Mount Gambier, on the South Australian side of the border, is built on the slopes of two of the largest craters, which now contain deep lakes.

The west coast of Victoria displays some of the most dramatic scenery in Australia. Massive beds of sandstone and limestone, formed on an ancient seabed now high above sea-level, are being cut into by the ocean, to produce towering vertical cliffs. In places, harder masses of rock have been left behind by the advancing sea, to form isolated stacks off the coast. One colourful group is known as the Twelve Apostles.

At Cape Otway and again at Wilson's Promontory, the southernmost point of the Australian mainland, very old weathered granite formations thrust into the ocean, still resisting the stormy seas that beat unceasingly against them. This wild stretch of coastline — broken only by Port Phillip Bay and Western Port Bay — was a notorious graveyard for ships in the early days of settlement.

LEFT: The Murray River, the trunk of the most extensive river system in Australia, winds through irrigated farmland in South Australia. Through its tributaries, which originate in four States, the Murray drains about one-sixth of the Australian continent.

LEFT: Franklin Harbour, a small inlet on Spencer Gulf, South Australia. The waters are so still and clear that weed growth on the sandy bottom appears almost exposed, although in fact it is covered by several metres of water.

ABOVE TOP: Whyalla, South Australia. This city had its origin in 1901 as a loading point for the large deposits of iron ore found at nearby Iron Knob. Originally the ore was shipped to Port Pirie, and later, from 1911, to Newcastle, New South Wales. In the early 1960s, however, steelworks and blast-furnaces were installed at Whyalla, and today the city produces a significant proportion of Australia's pig iron and steel ingots. Whyalla is also Australia's largest shipbuilding centre.

ABOVE: An open-air stockpile of steel billets at Whyalla.

RIGHT: Landscape near Port Pirie, South Australia. These broad plains east of Spencer Gulf have been farmed since the early days of the colony. They extend to the foothills of the Flinders Ranges, a rocky spine which runs north into the arid interior of the continent.

BELOW: Port Pirie. This busy industrial city near the head of Spencer Gulf was named after the ship *John Pirie*, which brought some of South Australia's first settlers from England. It began as a small settlement visited infrequently by sailing ships, but became an important shipping centre when wheat growing spread to the northern districts around the Gulf. Lead and zinc smelting, which began in 1889, is today the city's major industry.

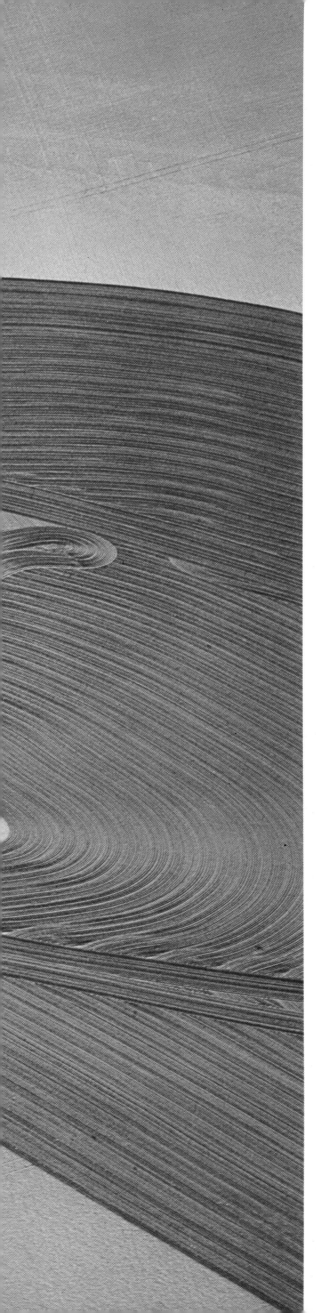

LEFT AND ABOVE: Patterns made by ploughing in preparation for the spring sowing on the bountiful wheatfields of Yorke Peninsula, South Australia.

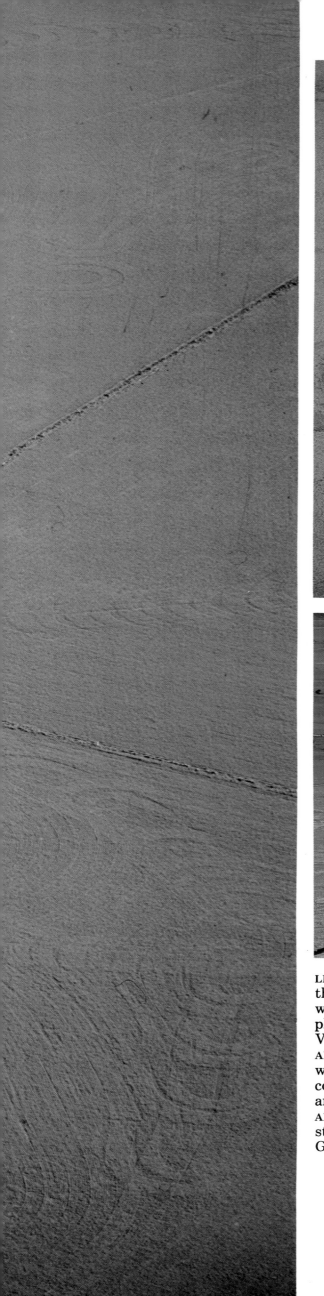

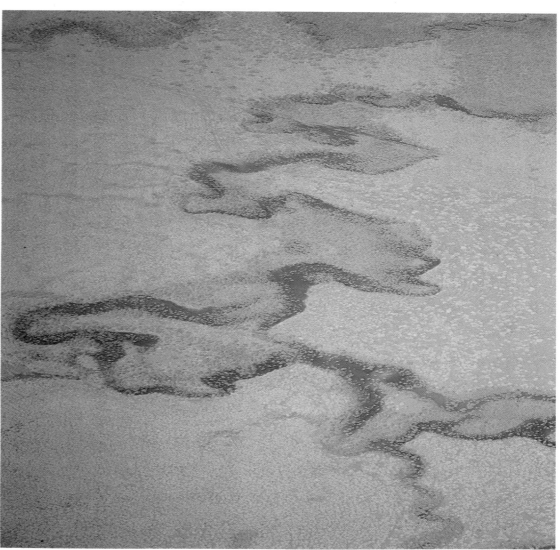

LEFT: Crops have been planted right to the margins of this eroded stream bed, which meanders across the coastal plain near Port Wakefield, on Gulf St Vincent, South Australia.

ABOVE TOP: A shallow watercourse has wound its way across low-lying country north of Adelaide, in search of an outlet to Gulf St Vincent.

ABOVE: Patches of yellow capeweed stain lush pastures near the head of Gulf St Vincent.

LEFT: Adelaide, capital of South Australia. The choice of a site for this city caused much dispute among the early settlers. Some, including the Governor, Captain John Hindmarsh, preferred Port Lincoln on the Eyre Peninsula, or the area near the mouth of the Murray River. The decision finally went to this site on Gulf St Vincent, chosen by the Surveyor General, Colonel William Light. Light's city plan, one of the most visionary in Australian history, aimed to prevent the civic centre from being swallowed up by the suburbs. He included a belt of parkland around the central area, and incorporated part of the course of the Torrens River (right of picture). Despite Adelaide's growth, this green "moat" survives. The Adelaide Cultural Centre is on the bank of the river (rear right).

BELOW: Vineyards at Magill, one of Adelaide's north-eastern suburbs. It was in this area, in 1844, that Doctor Rawson Penfold planted his first vines — the beginning of Penfold Wines, now one of Australia's best known wine companies.

OVERLEAF: After the winter rains, a low-lying area of Kangaroo Island, South Australia, is dimpled with clear pools. Sheep pick their way across the water-logged landscape, to graze on the rich pasture.

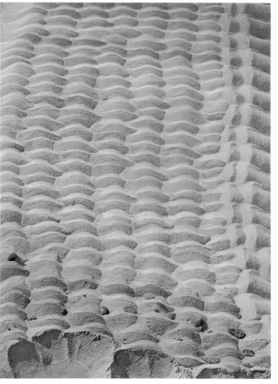

ABOVE: A lush landscape on Kangaroo Island, South Australia. The patchwork of green paddocks and tree-lined roads receding to the low hills is reminiscent of the English countryside, the birthplace of many of South Australia's first settlers.

ABOVE LEFT: Tilted beds of sedimentary rocks on Kangaroo Island. In geological terms, the island is a "horst", or flat-topped uplifted block. It is a continuation of the Flinders Ranges — Mount Lofty formation, but was cut off from the mainland some 7000 years ago by the rise in sea-level at the end of the last Ice Age.

LEFT: Geometrical patterns of an orchard, Kangaroo Island.

FAR LEFT: A decorative sand stockpile on Kangaroo Island.

LEFT: Warmed by the sun, the fissured rock platform at the south-western tip of Kangaroo Island provides a sanctuary for a colony of hair seals.
ABOVE: Admiralty Arch, on Cape du Couedic, Kangaroo Island. The Cape consists of a thick layer of limestone, overlying harder granite basement rock; pounding seas, slowly eroding the limestone, have produced this spectacular formation called Admiralty Arch. The hanging curtain of stalactites is produced by rainwater percolating through the limestone and dissolving mineral salts which recrystallise when exposed to the atmosphere.

59

FAR RIGHT: The Coorong, South Australia, a long shallow lagoon running parallel to the coast and separated from the sea by a thin spit called the Younghusband Peninsula. One of the most unusual waterways on the Australian coast, it extends nearly 150 kilometres, but never exceeds more than about 2 kilometres in width. Its existence is dependent on the Peninsula's barrier of low, vegetated sand dunes, which absorbs the onslaught of waves from the sea. The name Coorong is derived from an Aboriginal word meaning neck of water.

ABOVE: The calm, sheltered waters of the Coorong. This area provides ideal conditions for sailing, swimming, fishing and camping.

RIGHT: Towards its southern end, the Coorong becomes a string of increasingly salty lakes and saltpans. Part of the Coorong, lying between the road and the beach, forms Coorong National Park.

RIGHT: Near Nelson on the South
Australia—Victoria border, a farmer
has carefully ploughed between rocky,
tree-studded outcrops to create, on a
larger scale, the likeness of a
traditional Japanese garden of
immaculately raked gravel.
ABOVE: The textured carpet of a pine
plantation in South Australia, not far
from the Victorian border.

ABOVE: Mount Gambier, South Australia. The city is situated beside two large craters of an extinct volcano which, according to radio-carbon dating, was active as recently as 4700 years ago. The crater in the foreground has been turned into a park, with facilities for water sports.
RIGHT: This sinkhole near Mount Gambier was produced by the collapse of the roof of an underground cave.
FAR RIGHT, ABOVE: Portland, Victoria. Originally a whaling centre, Portland has been developed into the only deep water port between Melbourne and Adelaide.
FAR RIGHT, BELOW: Warrnambool, Victoria. The early history of this city, which began as a port, is commemorated by the two large sailing ships floating in the land-locked maritime museum (centre of picture).

LEFT: Port Campbell National Park, western Victoria. This part of the coastline is being rapidly eroded by the sea. The rocks are soft shales, sandstone and limestone laid down on an ancient sea floor and now uplifted as much as 150 metres above sea level. As the coast recedes, the undercut material collapses into the sea, leaving the spectacular vertical cliffs. Slightly harder masses of rock are left standing isolated, well away from the cliffs, in various stages of disintegration — some in large, solid blocks, others as tapering spires or low hummocks, already awash.

ABOVE: One of the Twelve Apostles, a group of large offshore sandstone stacks in Port Campbell National Park, Victoria. In time they will disappear beneath the waves, which are slowly undermining both them and the cliffs beyond.

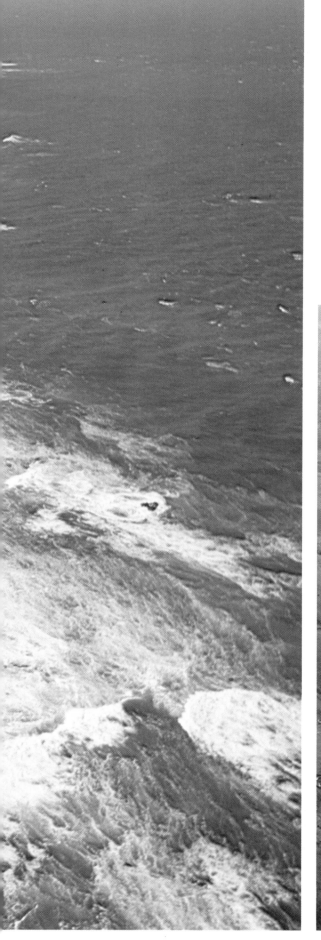

ABOVE LEFT: Cape Otway, Victoria. The
lighthouse, completed in 1848, was the
first on the Victorian coastline. It was
built to guide ships making their first
landfall on this stormy shore, after the
long voyage from England to the new
colonies.

ABOVE: Ford River weaves its way
through the Otway Ranges, which
lie close to the southern Victorian
coastline. The Otways are one of the
wettest parts of the State, with
rainfall in places exceeding 2000
millimetres a year.

LEFT: Lorne, one of several small
secluded holiday resorts tucked away
between the Otways and the sea.

RIGHT: Melbourne, capital of Victoria. This view from the south takes in Albert Park, one of the many green and pleasant open spaces in the inner city. Both the park and its ornamental lake were reclaimed from a swamp. The beach-front suburb in the foreground is St Kilda, which faces Port Phillip Bay.

ABOVE: Gently rolling country in the Kilmore district, north of Melbourne. In places the pastures show signs of erosion, caused by heavy grazing.

ABOVE: Melbourne's West Gate Bridge, which crosses the lower Yarra River to link Melbourne with its western suburbs. The bridge cost 200 million dollars and was opened in 1978.

LEFT: Melbourne, from near the mouth of the Yarra River. With a population of around two and a half million, Melbourne is Australia's second largest city.

ABOVE RIGHT: The tightly packed south-eastern suburbs of Melbourne are indicative of the city's explosive growth since World War II. In that time, the population has more than doubled.

OVERLEAF: Mornington Peninsula, which forms the eastern arm of Port Phillip Bay. Although rapidly becoming urbanised, the Peninsula retains rural activities such as dairying, fruit growing, and poultry, cattle and sheep farming.

FAR LEFT: The Rip, a fast and dangerous tidal flow through the narrow entrance to Port Phillip Bay (right of picture). In the early days many sailing ships found themselves in difficulties in the tide race, and even today, despite extensive blasting and dredging, ships find the passage a challenge.

ABOVE: Western Port Bay. This quiet sheet of water, south-east of Melbourne, has been the scene of prolonged dispute over proposed industrial development on its shores. State authorities now monitor the effects on the environment of discharges from refineries and other industrial plants.

LEFT: Newhaven (left of picture), a holiday resort on Phillip Island, which lies across the mouth of Western Port Bay. The area on the mainland opposite is San Remo.

LEFT: Wilson's Promontory, Victoria, a massive granite formation projecting into Bass Strait. First sighted by George Bass in 1798, it is named after Thomas Wilson, a prominent London merchant who was engaged in trade with Australia.

ABOVE: Looking towards Wilson's Promontory, from the mainland. Many thousands of years ago the Promontory was an island, but through wave action and various sea-level changes it has become joined to the mainland by the broad sand spit shown in the foreground.

OVERLEAF: A panoramic view of Wilson's Promontory. The southernmost point of the Australian mainland, the Promontory in places rises more than 600 metres. Its densely vegetated slopes support a rich variety of wildflowers and animal life. In earlier times, the bays were the haunts of sealers and whalers.

Tasmania and Bass Strait

Tasmania is the smallest State in Australia, but it possesses a great diversity of landforms, vegetation and climate, and this diversity is reflected in its coastline. There could hardly be a greater contrast between the broad sandy beaches of the north-east and the towering black cliffs of the south-west, or between the neat checkerboard farmlands of the north coast and the desolate windswept button-grass plains of the west coast.

Tasmania was once joined to the mainland by a mountain ridge, but it became isolated when the sea-level rose at the end of the last Ice Age. This cut the natural land-bridge to Tasmania and created Bass Strait. Today the stepping stones of the Kent and Furneaux island groups at the eastern entrance to Bass Strait, and Wilson's Promontory on the mainland, are all that can be seen of the ridge.

The north coast of Tasmania is rolling country. Generally low lying, much of it has been closely settled and farmed, and has a distinctly English appearance. In contrast, the rugged west coast remains almost as deserted as it was when the Dutch navigator Abel Tasman cautiously skirted its thunderous shores in 1642. Today the only town on the west coast is Strahan, on Macquarie Harbour.

Some of the most spectacular scenery in the world is to be seen in the south-western corner of Tasmania, where dramatic landforms have been produced by part of the land sinking into the sea. The ceaseless swells from the Southern Ocean have carved tremendous cliffs and caverns; particularly striking are towering walls of black dolerite, a basaltic rock which has formed clustered columns resembling organ pipes.

Sheltered in the long estuary of the Derwent River, at the south-east corner of the island, is Hobart, the Tasmanian capital. The city stands not far from the ruins of Port Arthur, the most evocative and best preserved reminder of Australia's convict era.

From the Tasman Peninsula, with its wave-cut and spray-filled chasms, the east coast becomes increasingly low and regular, and is studded with white sandy beaches and sheltered bays as far as Bass Strait.

LEFT: Cape Pillar, on the rugged south-eastern tip of Tasmania. This is part of the wildest coastline of the entire continent. Tasman Island (right) is named after the Dutch navigator Abel Tasman, who passed here in 1642.

LEFT: West Double Sandy Point, on the north coast of Tasmania. Unlike the rocky southern coastline this area, bordering Bass Strait, is generally low and sandy. Here, west of Bridport, the onshore winds have removed long strips of vegetation from the coastal dunes.

ABOVE TOP: Low Head, situated at the entrance to the Tamar River estuary.

ABOVE: Batman Bridge, near Launceston. Opened in 1968, this unusual cable-stayed truss bridge was the first permanent crossing over the Tamar River. It is named after John Batman, who in 1835 sailed from Launceston to acquire land at Port Phillip Bay, an event which led to the founding of Melbourne.

RIGHT: Launceston, the second largest city in Tasmania. The city lies about 68 kilometres from the sea, at the point where the North Esk River and the South Esk River join to form the Tamar River (left). In 1895 Launceston became one of the first towns in Australia to be supplied with electricity; power was generated by turbines in the Cataract Gorge (foreground).

ABOVE TOP The fertile black soil of the Tamar Valley, near Launceston, is exposed by the springtime ploughing.

ABOVE: Part of the Old Colonial Motor Inn, Launceston. Built in 1847, this handsome building was originally a schoolhouse.

LEFT: Drys Bluff, northern Tasmania.
Rising 1300 metres, the Bluff is part
of the Great Western Tiers, the
mighty north wall of Tasmania's
central tableland. This steep eroded
escarpment faces north-east and the
tableland slopes away to the south-
west, eventually disappearing beneath
the ocean in a long submarine ridge
that extends for hundreds of
kilometres.

ABOVE: A re-afforestation area,
south-east of Devonport. The
mountains on the horizon are part of
the Great Western Tiers.

ABOVE TOP: Inland from Devonport.
This area has been stripped of trees, to
supply timber for Tasmania's wood-
chip industry.

LEFT: Outskirts of Latrobe, near Devonport. These closely settled farmlands on Tasmania's north coast have a distinctly English appearance.

ABOVE: Devonport, at the mouth of the Mersey River. This port serves the prosperous fruit-growing and farming areas of the Mersey Valley and is the terminal for the Bass Strait vehicle and passenger ferry service from Melbourne.

ABOVE TOP: The cultivated fields in this patchwork landscape at Railton, near Devonport, are smaller than those generally found in Australia.

OVERLEAF: Table Cape, near Wynyard, on Tasmania's north coast. At some points along this part of the coastline, old volcanic vents have left plugs of basaltic rock standing high above the shoreline. To take advantage of the rich red soil which forms on such plugs, farms extend right to the edge of the cliffs.

LEFT: Stanley and the Nut. The small crayfishing town of Stanley is overshadowed by the Nut, the most impressive of the volcanic plugs left standing above the north Tasmanian shoreline. This formation — produced by an upwelling of molten basalt through a fault in the underlying rocks more than 10 million years ago — is the hard core of the volcano and became exposed when the surrounding landscape was subsequently worn down by erosion.

BELOW: Robbins Island, a coastal feature in Tasmania's north-west corner which is atypical of the shores of Bass Strait. The large, low-lying expanse of sand dunes enclosing clear, sandy channels of emerald water is more reminiscent of the tropics than of the southern seas.

LEFT: Albatross Island. This outcrop of black rock off the north-western tip of Tasmania is one of the few places in the world where the majestic sea-bird, the albatross, is known to breed; other areas are on remote islands close to the Antarctic continent. The lighter patches above the steep cliffs on the far side of the island are the rookeries of the white-capped albatross, a species which spends much of its life at sea, travelling huge distances in the wind currents that circulate around the South Pole.

BELOW LEFT: Thousands of albatross chicks sit in nests crowded together on the cliff-top rookery, waiting to be fed by the parent birds.

BELOW FAR LEFT: Trefoil Island. The rough and overgrown landing strip on this small island does not seem to have been used — except by sheep — since an aircraft ran off the runway and was abandoned.

BELOW AND BELOW RIGHT: Cape Grim, Tasmania. Beneath the winds of the "roaring forties" the melaleucas or paperbark trees on the coastal heathlands grow low and densely packed, resembling animal fur.

RIGHT: Ocean Beach, on Tasmania's west coast. This coastline is almost completely unpopulated, an unmarked seascape of broad beaches and rocky cliffs swept by the ceaseless winds and waves. It was along this coast that between 1832 and 1834 George Augustus Robinson contacted the last of Tasmania's tribal Aborigines and tried to persuade them to move to the new settlement on Flinders Island, where conditions were more favourable.

ABOVE: Emerging from the tumbled mountains of the central highlands, the Pieman River flows through an untouched wilderness to the desolate west coast. The Pieman was one of the last major rivers in Tasmania to be dammed for electricity generation.

LEFT: Hell's Gates. This is the entrance to Macquarie Harbour, one of the few large inlets on the west coast of Tasmania. It was named Hell's Gates because of the fierce tidal rips that pour through the narrow opening.

ABOVE TOP: Macquarie Harbour. This harbour is a drowned river valley and was created by the rise in sea level at the end of the last Ice Age. It extends inland for more than 30 kilometres, through rough, mountainous country.

ABOVE: In Macquarie Harbour the demarcation line between the normal harbour water (right) and the inflow from the heavily polluted King River (left) is clearly visible. The pollution is caused by copper mining operations.

RIGHT: Strahan, the only town on Tasmania's west coast. Standing on the north-western shore of Macquarie Harbour, the town was founded in 1878 to serve the silver-lead mine at Zeehan. It later served the Mount Lyell mine near Queenstown (which first mined gold, then silver, and finally copper). When Mount Lyell began shipping its copper by rail to Burnie on the north coast, Strahan began a slow decline. However it is now growing again with the prospect of increased tourism.

ABOVE: A small crayfishing fleet operates from Strahan.

LEFT: Settlement Island, Macquarie Harbour. Originally known as Sarah Island, this was the location of one of the most infamous convict settlements in Australia's history (and the chief inspiration for Marcus Clarke's novel *For the Term of His Natural Life*). It was established in 1822, on the orders of Governor Sorell, as a means of isolating intractable convicts from the main settlement at Hobart. The convicts were employed in building boats for government use, from the tall Huon pines along the Gordon River; the largest made was a barque of 200 tonnes. Flogging and ill-treatment were frequent, and the worst offenders were confined to the tiny island, seen beyond. The settlement was closed in 1834. Today the ruins are almost swallowed up in the trees.

ABOVE: The upper reaches of Macquarie Harbour.

RIGHT: After plunging down through steep gorges from the mountainous heart of south-western Tasmania, the Gordon River flows with unruffled beauty between densely forested banks. This stretch of the river will be affected by the Hydro-Electric Commission's plan to dam the lower Gordon.

BELOW: Thickly timbered hills at the head of Macquarie Harbour, with Mount Sorell in the background and the entrance to the Gordon River on the right.

ABOVE: Mountain ridges float like islands in a cloud-filled valley along the Gordon River, which flows into Macquarie Harbour on Tasmania's west coast.
LEFT: The upper reaches of the Gordon River.

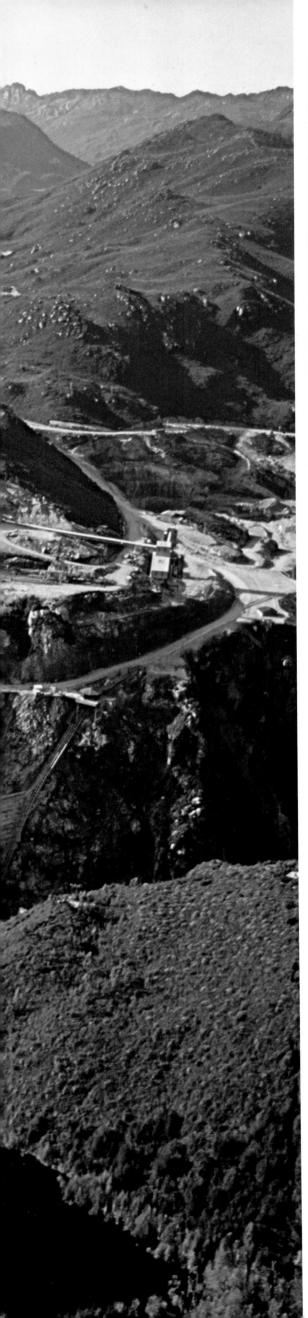

LEFT: The Lake Gordon hydro-electric power project, in south-western Tasmania. The thin, curved concrete structure in the foreground holds back the Gordon River to create the main storage capacity of the hydro-electric scheme. This project has caused much controversy both inside and outside Tasmania, with critics objecting not only to the disfiguring of the landscape by roads and other works, but more particularly to the flooding of Lake Pedder (background).

ABOVE: The township of Strathgordon, with man-made Lake Gordon in the background. The town was built in 1969 to house the workers on the Lake Gordon power project and is today used as a maintenance base by the Hydro-Electric Commission.

OVERLEAF: The new Lake Pedder. This great expanse of water was created by dams to provide reserve supplies for the nearby Lake Gordon power scheme. It covers the original Lake Pedder, which was a small but exquisite gem-like lake with a dazzling white beach.

FAR LEFT: The waters of the new Lake Pedder spread like an inland sea between the peaks of the Frankland Range (right) and Mount Anne and Mount Eliza (in the distance). An offshoot of the Frankland Range has almost become an island (centre).

ABOVE: Along the southern rim of Lake Pedder, the Frankland Range shows signs of the glaciation which affected parts of Tasmania during past Ice Ages. As the glaciers flowed downwards they gouged out the broad valleys, called cirques.

LEFT: The grinding of glaciers in the Frankland Range left the higher ridges of quartzite rock jagged and serrated, making them among the most inaccessible peaks on the Australian continent.

LEFT: Moulters Inlet, a quiet corner of Bathurst Harbour on the south-west corner of Tasmania.

BELOW: Bathurst Harbour. Created by rising sea levels at the end of the last Ice Age, this harbour winds almost 20 kilometres from the Southern Ocean (background), into the mountainous interior. In the past, whalers and passing ships sometimes sheltered in the secluded inlets. However the area is almost totally inaccessible by land and is still completely uninhabited.

RIGHT: South East Cape. Jutting into the heavy swells that roll up incessantly from the Southern Ocean, this headland creates surges and pressure waves in the boiling seas, making conditions extremely hazardous for boats that pass too close.

BELOW: South Cape, the southernmost tip of Tasmania. The scenery here illustrates the fate of a coastline that has sunk beneath the sea. The ocean assaults the remaining ridges, carving them into spectacular headlands and coves.

BELOW RIGHT: A crayfishing boat, laden with craypots, heads for the fishing grounds off southern Tasmania.

RIGHT: South Bruny Island (background), on Tasmania's south-east coast, is joined tenuously to North Bruny Island by a narrow sand spit created by wave action in Adventure Bay (left of picture). This now vegetated spit is strong enough to prevent the swells from breaking through to the more sheltered D'Entrecasteaux Channel (right). The "Siamese twin" islands were discovered in 1642 by the Dutch navigator Abel Tasman, but were not named for another 150 years, until the area was explored by Rear-Admiral Joseph Bruni d'Entrecasteaux.

ABOVE: Ghost forest, South Bruny Island. Because of its high rainfall this island supports some of the best forests in Tasmania. However these once mighty mountain ash were killed by bushfire.

OVERLEAF: Hobart, the capital of Tasmania. Founded in 1804 on a site about 20 kilometres upstream from the mouth of the Derwent River, Hobart is the second oldest capital city in Australia; only Sydney is older. The initial settlement party, under Lieutenant-Governor Colonel David Collins, numbered 262 people, about half of whom were convicts. The city grew steadily, mostly on the west bank (background), until the construction of the Tasman Bridge (centre right) in 1964 which encouraged the growth of the new suburbs (foreground).

RIGHT: Hobart. The city has grown up around Collins' settlement on Sullivan Cove, which is now the main port area. Although the city centre consists almost entirely of new buildings, some fine historic buildings erected before 1850 are preserved on Battery Point (left of picture).

ABOVE: Zinc refinery on the Derwent River. The problems of industrial development in rural areas are illustrated by this river, which is now so heavily polluted that the once renowned Derwent River oysters are no longer suitable for consumption. Measures to control discharge of wastes have been introduced but scientific studies suggest that the estuarine sediments will remain heavily contaminated for many years.

LEFT: Cape Raoul, on the extreme tip of Tasman Peninsula, offers some of the most spectacular coastal scenery in Tasmania. The dark vertical columns are black dolerite, forced to the surface from the earth's interior and spread like lava across large areas of Tasmania. A curious feature of dolerite is the way it cracks at right angles to the direction of flow, to produce this vertical columnar structure.

ABOVE: The main body of the dolerite formations at Cape Raoul rises nearly 200 metres above the sea.

127

RIGHT: Port Arthur, on the Tasman Peninsula, Tasmania's most popular tourist attraction. The ruins of this famous penal settlement, which is located 100 kilometres from Hobart, are the most extensive and best preserved relics of Australia's convict history. The settlement was established in 1830, and gradually grew into a large, self-supporting community which became the industrial centre for the whole colony of Van Diemen's Land. It was abandoned in 1877 and the buildings survived intact for 20 years, until a devastating bushfire swept through the settlement, gutting the wooden shingle roofs of most of the buildings. The church in the foreground was probably built by the convict architect James Blackburn; it has no name and was never consecrated. The large ruin (left) was a four-storey penitentiary. ABOVE: The Isle of the Dead, off Port Arthur. This tiny island was the burial place for convicts and soldiers stationed at the Port Arthur penal settlement. More than 1760 graves have been found; those of officers are marked with headstones, those of convicts are unmarked.

ABOVE LEFT: Cape Pillar, on the southeast tip of the Tasman Peninsula. The fluted cliffs are black dolerite.

ABOVE: The dolerite "organ pipes" of Cape Haùy on the Tasman Peninsula.

LEFT: Tasman's Arch, near Eaglehawk Neck which joins Tasman Peninsula to Forestier Peninsula. On several parts of this coastline the sea has worn its way deeply into the cliffs along fault lines. At Tasman's Arch the roof of a wave-worn cavern has collapsed, leaving a lofty arch bridging an awesome cavern. Visitors can peer straight down into it from the car park, or walk along a narrow path to the seaward side.

RIGHT: St Helens. This small town on Tasmania's north-east coast was a busy centre at the turn of the century when thousands of small alluvial tin mines operated in the area. In more recent times the dairying industry dominated the district, but with the post-war drift to the cities the population began a slow decline. Today the town is a crayfishing port, and its fleet ranks fifth in Tasmania in the size of its catch.

ABOVE: Environmental scars of Tasmania's wood-chip industry. Large areas of eucalypt forest on Tasmania's east coast have been logged for wood-chipping. After clear-felling, sloping areas such as this are prone to erosion, especially along the roads and tracks used to haul the logs to transports.

FAR LEFT: The massive granite walls of the Strzelecki Peaks on Flinders Island reflect the history of this and other islands in the Furneaux and Kent groups. Strung across Bass Strait between north-east Tasmania and Wilson's Promontory in Victoria, these islands are all that is left of a ridge that connected Tasmania to the mainland about 15,000 years ago.
BELOW: Whitemark, a small resort and fishing centre on Flinders Island.
TOP LEFT: The Kent Group in Bass Strait, rugged islands of very old rocks which are now deeply cut into by the sea.
LEFT: Chappell Island, in the Furneaux Group. This island is renowned among zoologists as the home of a large and almost black sub-species of the mainland tiger snake, with a remarkably potent venom.

Wilson's Promontory to Fraser Island

The south-east coast is one of the most varied and attractive regions of Australia. Its character is dominated by the Great Divide, an almost continuous belt of highlands which extends up the entire east coast to Cape York. These uplands plunge steeply to a narrow coastal plain. The rivers on this eastern watershed are generally short and fast-flowing, and many have cut deep gorges and valleys to the sea. Some of the valleys have been drowned by the sea, producing spectacular harbours such as Port Jackson and Broken Bay.

From Port Albert, on Victoria's south-east coast, the remarkably straight and unbroken line of Ninety Mile Beach runs almost to the New South Wales border. Behind the beach's frontal dunes lie the Gippsland Lakes, sheltered waterways that have become popular holiday resorts.

The entire New South Wales coastal plain is narrow, and highlands rise abruptly within sight of the sea. Picturesque sandy beaches alternate with sheer rocky cliffs and headlands, even within the ocean-front suburbs of Sydney, the capital city of New South Wales.

North of Newcastle lie the Myall Lakes, another chain of freshwater lakes separated from the sea by broad sand dunes, some of which are richly forested. In their tranquil and unspoiled beauty, they surpass even the Gippsland Lakes.

Once into Queensland the boundary between the temperate south-east and the tropical north-east coast is marked by a group of great sand islands: Moreton and North and South Stradbroke off Brisbane, and Fraser Island further north. They are beautiful and unique. Fraser Island is the world's largest island made entirely of sand, and the crest of Moreton Island is the highest sand ridge in existence. All the islands have an impressive diversity of vegetation. Their dunes contain minerals, and this has led to extended controversy between mining interests and environmentalists over the question of mining on the islands.

LEFT: The dramatic anchor formation of Barrenjoey Head north of Sydney, with Pittwater on the right. Once an island, Barrenjoey Head is now joined by a sand spit to Palm Beach on the mainland.

BELOW: Corner Inlet, Victoria. Tucked in behind the bulwark of Wilson's Promontory (background, left of picture), Corner Inlet is sheltered from the stormy seas and currents of the Tasman Sea (left) by the maze of low sand and mud islands just inside the entrance.

RIGHT: The sand banks and shallow channels of Corner Inlet.

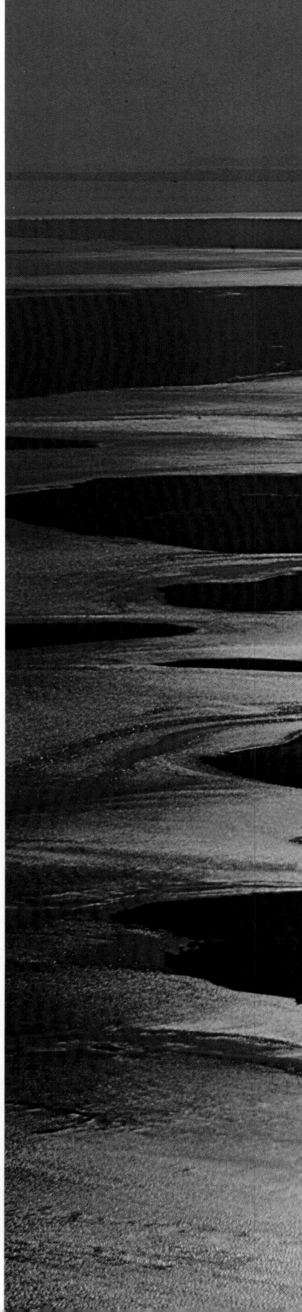

LEFT: The low, rolling hills near Woodside in south-eastern Victoria enclose many lush valleys which have been turned into profitable farmlands and dairy properties.

ABOVE TOP: Patterns of plant growth in the shallow freshwater lakes behind the Ninety Mile Beach.

ABOVE: Streams feeding the coastal lakes wind across the marshy flats.

LEFT: Ninety Mile Beach, Victoria.
This extremely long and straight sand
spit has been created by the prevailing
onshore winds and waves. Trapped
behind it is a series of river-fed
freshwater lakes. Small settlements
along the beach are popular with
beach fishermen and holidaymakers.
BELOW: The sheltered lakes and
lagoons behind the Ninety Mile Beach
are a haven for waterbirds.
BOTTOM: A solitary traveller on the
Ninety Mile Beach.

RIGHT: Lakes Entrance, Victoria. This single narrow break in the coastal dunes provides the only connection between the Tasman Sea and the Gippsland Lakes.

ABOVE TOP: Barracouta rig, Bass Strait. This production platform has been developed, together with the nearby Marlin platform, to supply natural gas to Melbourne; together the two fields have reserves for about 20 years.

ABOVE: Paynesville, one of several holiday resorts on the Gippsland Lakes which give access to large stretches of water ideal for boating, swimming and fishing.

144

ABOVE: Cann River estuary, Victoria. Towards the New South Wales border the eastern uplands swing close to the coast, and a number of rivers cut their way through to the sea. The Cann River empties across a broad sand bar.
ABOVE RIGHT: Running almost 60 kilometres between Lakes Entrance and Marlo is one of the longest unbroken stretches of beach on the entire east coast.
RIGHT: Deep in the sedge-covered lakes behind Ninety Mile Beach, a black swan sits on the nest it has built from the surrounding plants.

ABOVE: Mallacoota Inlet, Victoria.
Where the Genoa River enters the sea,
near the New South Wales border, this
deep inlet winds through the hills
between thickly wooded banks.

FAR LEFT: Gale force winds from the
Tasman Sea have in places carved
"blow-outs" in the vegetated coastal
dunes of Mallacoota Inlet.

LEFT: Point Hicks, Victoria. This was
Captain Cook's first landfall on the
Australian mainland during his
historic voyage along the east coast in
1770.

RIGHT: Cape Howe, on the Victoria—
New South Wales border.
BELOW: As evening approaches, a
fisherman heads for home towards
Mallacoota Inlet.

RIGHT: Disaster Bay, New South Wales, looking back towards Cape Howe. On this part of the coastline the highlands run close to the shore and a dense eucalypt forest grows to the edge of the beach.

ABOVE: Sea fog engulfs the coast, north of Cape Howe. Fogs are unusual off the east coast, but they sometimes form when a warm, moist airstream from the north meets a cold sea current flowing up the coast from Bass Strait.

ABOVE: Almost every inlet and estuary along the south coast of New South Wales has a town or settlement. This is Merimbula, a centre for game fishing.

TOP RIGHT: Tathra, a small town near Merimbula, built around a short beach between rocky headlands.

CENTRE RIGHT: Bermagui, a popular fishing and holiday resort on the south coast of New South Wales. In the 1930s the waters off Bermagui were world famous big game fishing grounds and attracted such renowned anglers as Zane Grey.

RIGHT: The Bega River drains one of the richest dairying and pastoral districts on the south coast of New South Wales. The town of Bega lies a few kilometres inland, behind the low ridge of hills.

OVERLEAF: Narooma, a typical and picturesque example of the river mouth settlements on the south coast of New South Wales. The town was originally called Noorooma, a local Aboriginal word for "blue water".

LEFT: Kiama, New South Wales. This little township sits beside a rugged point into which the sea has carved many fissures, including a now famous blow-hole (left side of point, in front of car park). The small but sheltered harbour was discovered by George Bass during his exploration of the south coast in 1797, and was used by cedar-cutters as early as 1815.

ABOVE: A mined point, north of Kiama. At various places along the coast, both south and north of Sydney, early navigators noticed black layers in the coastal cliffs. These were outcrops of a vast coal bed extending from Wollongong in the south to Newcastle in the north, and westward under the Blue Mountains. Being comparatively easy to work, these outcrops were mined early in the colony's history.

RIGHT: Port Kembla steelworks and loading wharves, New South Wales. Originally developed in 1883 as a harbour for shipping coal from the nearby Mount Kembla mine in the Illawarra Range, Port Kembla has grown into Australia's largest steel-making centre. Today the complex includes five blast furnaces and thirteen open-hearth steel furnaces, employs more than 20,000 workers and has a total capacity of 5.5 million tonnes of steel ingot a year.

ABOVE TOP: Mining of the coal seams on the New South Wales coast continues even today, although the major extraction of coal is now made from inland areas.

ABOVE: A bulk ore carrier rides at anchor off Port Kembla.

LEFT: Wollongong, the seventh largest city in Australia. With a population of approximately 200,000 this city sprawls across the coastal plain between the sea and the Illawarra Range, taking in Port Kembla and a number of other towns and settlements which have now merged. Like many places on the south coast it has only a small harbour in the lee of a rocky headland.

ABOVE TOP: The scalloped coastline, looking south towards Wollongong. Each beach has a small holiday resort.

ABOVE: The Southern Freeway sweeps along the edge of the Illawarra escarpment near Bulli Pass.

163

LEFT: The crumbling, layered walls of these sandstone cliffs near Wattamolla, south of Sydney, together with the wave-cut rock platforms at their base, form a spectacular part of the Royal National Park. The huge blocks of fallen rock illustrate the way the waves are undercutting the cliffs. Covering some 15,000 hectares of rugged coastal country on the southern outskirts of Sydney, the park was established in 1879 and was the second national park in the world, being authorised only seven years after Yellowstone in the United States of America.

ABOVE TOP: Campers at Royal National Park, near Garie Beach.

ABOVE: Garie Beach nestles in a small cove on the rugged coastline of the Royal National Park.

ABOVE RIGHT: Rough seas off the Royal National Park. Although dangerous, these waters are among the most popular fishing grounds south of Sydney.

165

RIGHT: Bondi Beach, Sydney, the best known surfing beach in Australia. The name is an abbreviation of the Aboriginal word "boondi", meaning "the noise of tumbling waves". Today the large pavilion facing the beach is used as a theatre.

ABOVE: The cliff-top cemetery at Bronte forms a stark foreground to the suburbs and distant commercial centre of Sydney.

OVERLEAF: Sydney, capital of New South Wales and the largest and oldest city in Australia. The first settlement of Australia was made here, at Sydney Cove (immediately behind the Sydney Opera House), in 1788, by a party of soldiers and convicts under Governor Arthur Phillip. The site was never officially named, but took its name from the cove, which was called Sydney Cove after the then Home Secretary, Viscount Sydney. Government House, completed in 1845, stands amid trees behind the Opera House.

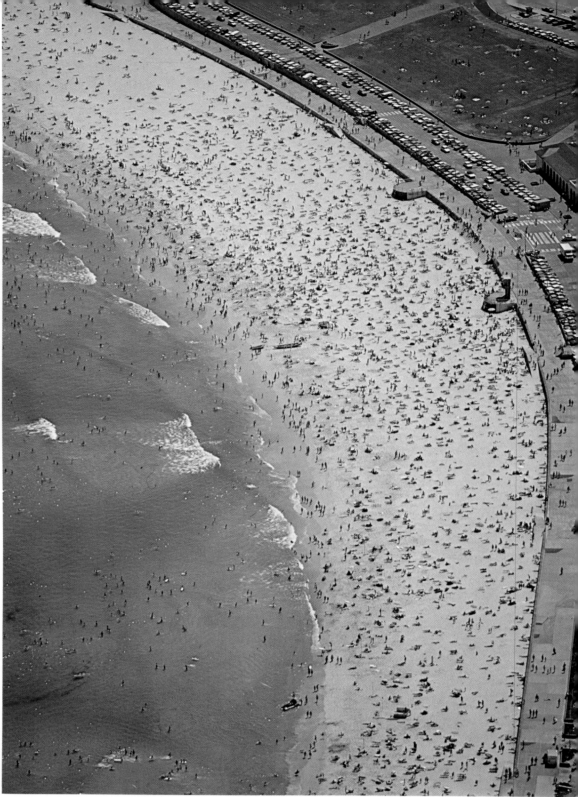

THIS PAGE: Sydney is a coastal city with a warm, sunny climate, as is evident by its residents' pre-occupation with outdoor recreations such as swimming, surfing, boating, sunbathing and hang-gliding.

OVERLEAF: The Barrenjoey Peninsula, with its series of crescent beaches, stretches away towards Broken Bay. Pittwater is seen at the left.

LEFT: In the quiet backwater of Ettalong, near Woy Woy, New South Wales, new waterside housing sites have been established on reclaimed land.

ABOVE: Gosford, at the northern end of Brisbane Water, near Sydney, is the heart of an extensive holiday and tourist area; it also has many residents who commute daily by train to Sydney, a distance of 81 kilometres. Surveyed and named in 1839, the city has a rich historic background. Today its chief link with the past is a museum of local history, located in a cottage where the poet Henry Kendall once lived.

ABOVE: The Entrance, New South Wales. The name of this tourist and commercial fishing centre was adopted because of its location beside the entrance to Tuggerah Lake, a large freshwater lake separated from the Tasman Sea by a narrow sand spit.

ABOVE RIGHT: Sand mining at Lake Munmorah, New South Wales. The dunes along much of the east coast contain minerals such as rutile and zircon. These are extracted by scooping up the sand with dredges and passing it through a mobile processing plant.

RIGHT: Toukley, south of Newcastle, is an example of the way that settlements on the east coast have developed on every suitable site between the sea and the coastal lakes.

OVERLEAF: Newcastle. With a population of just over 250,000, this is the sixth largest city in Australia. The main business centre is on the south bank of the Hunter River.

ABOVE: A few kilometres north of Newcastle the character of the coastline changes abruptly, with the industrialised areas giving way to the clean, sweeping sand dunes of Newcastle Bight.

LEFT: Newcastle's prosperity is based on coal and steel. Extensive coal deposits were discovered nearby as early as 1797, and in 1801 coal shipped from here to Bengal and Cape Town became Australia's first overseas exports. From 1801 until about 1824, the coal mines were occasionally used as a place of punishment for convicts who committed offences after being transported to Australia. There was a steady expansion of coal mining at Newcastle throughout the nineteenth century. A further, and significant, development came in 1911, when the Broken Hill Proprietary Company decided to establish its first steelworks at Newcastle.

ABOVE LEFT: A tranquil passage between two of the main arms of the Myall Lakes, New South Wales. Lake Boolambayte (left) and Myall Lake (right) are part of the chain of lakes now included in the Myall Lakes National Park.

ABOVE RIGHT: The Myall River drains the Myall Lakes and empties into the sea at Port Stephens.

LEFT: Sand mining operations on the dunes south of Myall Lake. Successive State governments have continued to allow sand mining inside the Myall Lake National Park, despite protests from many quarters.

FAR LEFT: Streamers of foam raised by wind blowing across Myall Lake.

RIGHT: The large and fairly shallow Smith's Lake, adjoining Myall Lake, is fed by freshwater streams. It never becomes very brackish because its mouth is often closed for long periods, being re-opened only by heavy seas and high tides.

BELOW: Sand mining near Smith's Lake, New South Wales. The sand mining activities which have aroused the greatest protest are those involving dunes such as these. Up to 120 metres high, they are clothed in unusually rich forests of angophora and blackbutt, large trees which are not normally found growing on pure sand. Critics argue that even if the contours of the dunes are restored after mining, the forests cannot be re-established.

LEFT: Sugarloaf Point lighthouse, built on a steep and rocky headland at the northern end of the Myall Lakes National Park.
ABOVE: North from Sugarloaf Point the coastline becomes increasingly rugged. The massive humps of Charlotte Head can be seen in the distance.

RIGHT: The fishing centre and holiday resort of Forster, New South Wales, lies beside the narrow entrance to Wallis Lake. Such entrances to coastal lakes are kept open by dredging, and provide shelter for boats wanting to escape the dangers of the open coastline.

ABOVE: Charlotte Head consists of an ancient mass of rock which is somewhat harder than the surrounding coastline. Resisting erosion, it has been left standing well above sea-level. It now forms the seaward bastion of Wallis Lake (left background).

OVERLEAF: Laurieton, situated about half-way between Taree and Port Macquarie, is typical of the scores of towns and settlements that crowd the narrow coastal plain on the east coast of Australia.

LEFT: Near Port Macquarie the coastal plain broadens, and patches of intensively worked farmland begin to appear. The rich soil on the flood plains of rivers, together with the ample rainfall, make the northern New South Wales coast very productive.

ABOVE TOP: The holiday resort of Nambucca Heads lies at the mouth of the Nambucca River, which rises in the precipitous New England plateau, close to the coast. The district was first settled by timber-getters in 1842, and the name of the settlement was taken from a local Aboriginal word meaning "entrance to the waters". The climate is favourable for the cultivation of fruit and vegetables.

ABOVE: The growing popularity of the northern New South Wales coast is reflected in the rapid expansion of places like Crescent Head, which until recent years consisted of only a handful of fishermen's shacks.

ABOVE LEFT: Dense stands of sugar
cane on the rich alluvial soil beside the
Richmond River, northern New South
Wales.

LEFT: The once sleepy holiday resort
of Surfers Paradise, Queensland, is
now the heart of the Gold Coast,
Australia's most popular coastal play-
ground. High-rise blocks of
apartments are steadily spreading
northwards and displacing the
traditional seaside bungalows.

ABOVE: North of Surfers Paradise, on
the Broadwater, the Sea World enter-
tainment complex features artificial
lakes where dolphins and water-ski
troupes perform.

OVERLEAF: The business centre of
Brisbane, Queensland's State capital,
and the Botanic Gardens beyond, lie in
a loop of the Brisbane River.

195

LEFT: Mount Coonowrin (Crookneck), Queensland. This towering rock spire is the core of an extinct volcano, one of a group which makes up the Glass House Mountains, north of Brisbane. They were formed some 20 million years ago when molten rock forced its way to the surface, making large volcanic cones and spraying the landscape with ash and lava. Eventually the core rock cooled and plugged the volcanic vents. Since then the surrounding cones have worn away, leaving massive plugs standing high above the landscape.

ABOVE: The Glass House Mountains. When Captain Cook was anchored in Moreton Bay in 1770 he glimpsed a number of peaks rising above the coastal plain to the north. A rainstorm had made their summits glisten like glass. Cook noted this in his log, and named them the Glass House Mountains.

RIGHT: Fraser Island, Queensland. The largest sand island in the world, it illustrates the unceasing struggle between the wind, which keeps the sand moving, and the vegetation, which tries to hold and stabilise it. Here the wind is getting the upper hand, driving waves of sand inland. In 1977 opponents of sand mining won a long battle to persuade the Australian Government to ban exports of minerals from Fraser Island, to preserve its unique character and vegetation.

ABOVE TOP: Moreton Island is one of three large islands of sand off the southern Queensland coast. On the seaward side some of the processes by which such islands grow can be seen. The sea has raised a low frontal dune some way out from the older, higher dunes. The new dune is being colonised and stabilised by plants, and eventually the enclosed lagoon will be filled in, building out the edge of the island.

ABOVE: The wreck of the *Cherry Venture,* north of Noosa Head.

The Capricorn Group to Lizard Island

The coast of Queensland differs from other parts of the coastline in several ways: it is the only portion of Australia's tropical region that is at all intensively populated; it has many picturesque islands scattered along its length; and it is protected by the world's greatest coral reef system.

The many islands lying close inshore are composed of the same kind of rocks as the mainland, and have clearly been cut off by the sea at some stage, either by a general subsidence of the coastline or by a rise in sea level, or perhaps by a combination of both. Many of the islands are strikingly beautiful, their sheer sides rising straight from the sea with a rich green covering of rainforest. Perhaps the best known group are those along the Whitsunday Passage; they include the popular resort islands of Hayman, Daydream, South Molle, Lindeman, and Whitsunday itself.

The outstanding feature of the Queensland coast is undoubtedly the Great Barrier Reef system. It is best described as a system because it consists of many different kinds of coral formations, contained within an Outer Barrier.

The Barrier Reef system is protected by an Outer Barrier, which runs along the edge of the continental shelf, where it forms a buffer against the swells of the Pacific Ocean. In the south the Outer Barrier consists of intermittent reefs, up to 320 kilometres from the coast, but further north it becomes an almost continuous wall, which in places comes to within 12 kilometres of the shore.

Between the Outer Barrier and the shore the sea floor is almost flat, shelving gradually towards the coast, and the water is rarely more than about 30 metres deep. Within this vast sheltered lagoon there are thousands of coral reefs and islands. Although attractive in appearance, and in some cases quite densely vegetated, the coral islands lack water and only two of them, Green Island and Heron Island, are permanently inhabited.

On the mainland, where the Queensland coastal plain widens, rich alluvial soil deposited by the State's many large rivers permits intensive agriculture, especially of sugar. Australia is the world's fourth-ranking sugar producing nation, and 95 per cent of the crop is grown along the Queensland coast.

LEFT: Coral patterns in the shallow
lagoon of a platform reef in the
Capricorn Group, at the southern end
of the Great Barrier Reef system.

LEFT: Erskine Island, in the
Capricorn Group. This low, wooded
islet is typical of the many islands
which have formed on platform reefs
between the Outer Barrier and the
mainland. The reefs are built by coral
polyps to a level which may be just
awash at low tide. The prevailing
winds and waves gradually build a cay
from broken coral and sand, usually
towards the leeward end of the reef.
Although such a cay is rarely more
than a metre or so above the high-
water level it can be colonised by
drifting seeds and fertilised by birds,
until eventually it can support a
luxuriant forest of trees, palms, vines
and other plants.
BELOW: Coral growths show up vividly
against the sandy bottom of the
crystal clear lagoon at One Tree Island
in the Capricorn Group.

ABOVE: One Tree Island, Capricorn Group. This small vegetated cay is the base for a program of scientific research on corals, reef growth, cay development and colonisation by plants and animals.

ABOVE: Heron Island, Capricorn Group. This and Green Island, near Cairns, are the only coral islands off the Queensland Coast to be developed as tourist resorts. Heron Island is world renowned for the colourful corals and fish that can be seen by snorkelling or scuba diving, or by walking out on the reef flats at low tide.

ABOVE RIGHT: A giant manta ray cruises lazily through the waters near Heron Island.

RIGHT: Holiday activities around the reefs at Heron Island. The boat on the left is being used as a tender by divers and snorkellers, while the boat with the canopy has a glass bottom, and is used for viewing the coral and fish.

RIGHT: The coastal flats of Cape Keppel, Queensland, are periodically inundated by the tide. Salt-tolerant mangroves are the only vegetation that can survive on them.

ABOVE: Round Hill Head, south of Gladstone. In some places along this part of the coast the tidal channels and their fringe of mangroves extend quite a way inland, behind the coastal ridges. The lighter patches are salt crusts, formed on top of the mud and silt after high tide.

LEFT: Rockhampton, the principal city of central Queensland. Located on the Fitzroy River, this city is the service centre for a vast pastoral and mining area, which includes the Mount Morgan gold and copper mine. It began its history in 1853 with one store and an inn, but grew rapidly after gold was discovered nearby in 1858. The city's largest secondary industry is meat processing.

ABOVE: During high tide the Fitzroy River spreads across its broad flood plain near Rockhampton.

OVERLEAF: Canefields near Sarina. The area between Sarina and Mackay is one of the richest sugar-producing districts in Queensland. Sugar cane was brought to Australia in 1788 from South Africa by the First Fleet, but large-scale cultivation did not begin until 1864, near Brisbane. The industry spread rapidly up the coast, and the first crushing mill in the Mackay district began working in 1866.

LEFT: The Cumberland Group, Queensland. These rocky islands extend along the coast from Mackay to Proserpine, forming a passage between them and the mainland. Captain Cook discovered the passage on Whitsunday, 1770, and named it, and the largest island in the group, in honour of that day.

BELOW FAR LEFT: Hayman Island. The accommodation area of this popular holiday resort at the northern end of Whitsunday Passage is built on the only flat area on the island. The reservoir behind the buildings contains fresh water, which is always scarce on these islands.

BELOW CENTRE LEFT: Pentecost Island (foreground) and Shaw Island in the Cumberland Group are steep and thickly wooded, and typical of the whole group. Once part of the mainland, they are the tips of hills which have been isolated by the rising sea-level.

BELOW LEFT: Brampton Island, a resort beside Whitsunday Passage, has a broad sheltered beach in one of its steep-sided bays.

BELOW: Fishing boats at anchor off Orpheus Island.

RIGHT: The actively developing delta of the Burdekin River, Queensland, which enters the Coral Sea south of Townsville, is one of the very few examples of this kind of coast formation in Australia. Generally, the Australian coastline lacks the deltas which mark the mouths of large rivers on other continents. The reason for this is that on many parts of the coast the ocean is too deep to permit the accumulation of silt required for delta construction, and powerful ocean waves and currents distribute the material along the coast before it can build up. The Burdekin, however, is developing multiple mouths, and parts of its delta have been colonised by vegetation.

BELOW: Sandbanks at the point where the ocean (left) meets the outflow of the Burdekin River mark the edge of the growing delta, and show how the material carried down by the river is slowly accumulating.

ABOVE LEFT: Magnetic Island, near Townsville, Queensland. Although some of the flatter areas of this island have been developed into holiday centres, the more remote parts still remain as untouched as they were when Captain Cook sailed past in the *Endeavour*. Cook gave the island its name because he believed that it had affected his ship's compasses.

FAR LEFT: Palm Island Aboriginal settlement, which was established by the Queensland Government in 1918 to accommodate Aborigines from the mainland. During its early use the settlement acquired a notorious reputation for the restrictions it placed on the inhabitants.

LEFT: Townsville, the major city of north Queensland. As well as serving pastoral, sugar-growing and mining areas, Townsville is the home of Queensland's second university, which is named after Captain James Cook, and of the Australian Institute of Marine Science, an important centre for research into the Great Barrier Reef and tropical waters.

OVERLEAF: Canefields near Ingham. The rich black alluvial soil deposited in the valley of the Herbert River, watered by the heavy tropical rainfall, makes this one of the most productive areas in Australia.

LEFT: Hinchinbrook Island. Measuring 35 kilometres long and up to 24 kilometres wide, this is the largest island along the Queensland coast. Its craggy peaks rise more than 1000 metres above the sea. When Captain Cook sighted the island he thought it was part of the mainland, and named it Mount Hinchinbrook. It was not until 1819, nearly 50 years later, that it was found to be an island.

ABOVE TOP: Even the steepest slopes of Hinchinbrook Island are covered with luxuriant rain forest, making exploration extremely difficult.

ABOVE: Mangroves on Hinchinbrook Island. The tangled roots of the mangroves (exposed at low tide) are a prolific breeding ground for fish and crustaceans. The net suspended between the mangroves to collect falling leaves has been placed there as part of a study of the productivity of this environment by the Australian Institute of Marine Science in Townsville.

OVERLEAF: Hinchinbrook Channel, between the island and the mainland (left of picture).

225

ABOVE: Cairns, north Queensland. This city is one of Australia's major sugar-shipping ports, and the centre for north Queensland's tourist traffic.
ABOVE RIGHT: The main street of Cooktown. For a period in the 1870s this was a busy town, following the discovery of gold on the Palmer River.
CENTRE RIGHT: Cook's Pillar, Cooktown. This stone monolith marks the spot on the banks of the Endeavour River where Captain Cook beached the *Endeavour* for repairs in 1770, after running aground on the Barrier Reef.
RIGHT: Daintree River, north Queensland. Rising in the highlands (background) the Daintree flows through verdant rain forest country before entering the sea through its mangrove-lined estuary.

LEFT: Canefields near Cairns, north Queensland. The rich red soils are extremely fertile, having been produced by the weathering of basalt, which in the past flowed from volcanoes all along this coast. The reddish colouring is due to a high content of iron.

BELOW: Burning cane waste after ploughing. When the ripening cane (foreground) is ready for harvest it will be burned to remove the leaves and other plant debris, making it easier to harvest the fire-resistant cane stems.

LEFT: The clear waters of the lagoons off Lizard Island (left of picture), north-east of Cooktown, contain a wealth of corals, giant clams and fish.
ABOVE: Looking seawards from Lizard Island. This high granite island lies near the Outer Barrier, which in this area runs close to the coast. The summit in the foreground is known as "Cook's Look", because Captain Cook climbed it in 1770, looking for a way out through the Outer Barrier, which had forced the *Endeavour* into increasingly shallow and dangerous waters.

ABOVE: The Outer Barrier, near Lizard Island. The opening visible in the middle distance is Cook's Passage, commonly believed to be the one through which Captain Cook escaped from inside the Great Barrier Reef.

RIGHT, TOP: Green Island, off Cairns.

RIGHT, CENTRE: Low Isles, north-east of Cairns. This tiny islet was the base for an historic British scientific expedition led by Sir Maurice Yonge in 1928-9 to collect corals from the Great Barrier Reef.

RIGHT: Murdock Island, off the coast near Cooktown, is a typical drowned hilltop.

Princess Charlotte Bay to Roper River

Cape York Peninsula and the Gulf of Carpentaria form one of the least known and most intriguing parts of the continent. Because the Peninsula is an almost roadless wilderness, and the shores of the Gulf are marshy and impassable during the wet season, this whole region remains largely unvisited and is still only sparsely populated.

Cape York Peninsula is a continuation of the mountainous ridge of the Great Divide, and the highlands continue almost to the tip. East of the Peninsula the Outer Barrier reef runs parallel to the coast and quite close to it, eventually breaking up in a maze of reefs and channels at the eastern end of Torres Strait.

The scores of islands in Torres Strait are of three kinds: the cones of extinct volcanoes, such as the Murray group, well out in the Coral Sea; the low coral islands between Cape York Peninsula and New Guinea; and the rocky continental islands close to the Peninsula, such as Thursday and Friday Islands.

On the western side of Cape York Peninsula, the shores of the Gulf of Carpentaria are low-lying. The only inhabitants are to be found at three Aboriginal settlements, a few remote cattle stations, and the bauxite mine at Weipa. The little township of Karumba, at the south-east corner of the Gulf of Carpentaria, is the base for a prawning fleet, which fishes the Gulf during the season, and for the barramundi fishermen, who spread their nets in the mouths of the rivers.

The southern shores of the Gulf are flat and featureless. Large rivers wind sluggishly across the tidal flats, inscribing elaborate patterns of blue water, brown mud, white salt and green mangroves. Beyond, the grassy plains stretch endlessly, a low gateway to the heart of the continent. The land here has been raised only very slightly since the time, more than 70 million years ago, when the Gulf extended right across the continent and linked up with the Southern Ocean.

LEFT: Normanby River, Queensland. Snaking its way towards Princess Charlotte Bay, the Normanby is a good example of a tropical drainage system.

LEFT: Morehead River, Queensland. The characteristic "tree" patterns of drainage on tropical river estuaries have a white background of salt crust on top of the underlying silt and sand. Where the outflow of water has cut channels, rich mud provides a foothold for the encroaching mangroves, which grow along the arms of the channels like bacteria invading the blood vessels of some organic system.

BELOW: The extraordinary wanderings of a single drainage channel, Morehead River. The mangroves are dependent upon the water and nutrients in the channel itself, as they cannot survive on the surrounding salt crust.

LEFT: Lockhart River, on the east coast of Cape York Peninsula, Queensland. The broad channels and sandbanks of this river are the haunts of the estuarine or saltwater crocodile. Valued for their skins, this species was almost wiped out before a hunting ban was imposed in the mid-1970s.

ABOVE: Lockhart River Mission. The transitional improvement in housing standards for the inhabitants of this mission is clearly shown in this picture (from left background to right foreground).

RIGHT: Cape York, Queensland, the northernmost tip of the Australian continent. This view looks back towards the mainland, showing Eborac Island in the foreground. Throughout the prehistory of Australia, Cape York and the chain of islands linking it with New Guinea were an important route of entry into the continent for plants, animals and people, particularly when sea levels were lower and Torres Strait was dry.

ABOVE: Princess Charlotte Bay. On the tidal flats, patches of harder material, partly consolidated by plants, survive like islands in a dry sea.

ABOVE TOP: The sandbanks are barely exposed at low tide in Princess Charlotte Bay.

ABOVE: Thursday Island (foreground). This island was once the centre of a flourishing industry in pearls, pearlshell, trochus shell and bêche-de-mer, but today its economic mainstay is fishing, prawning and crayfishing. The population is about 2500, the majority of whom are Torres Strait Islanders. (Hammond Island is in the centre of the picture and Goode Island on the far left.)

FAR LEFT: A pearling lugger on the beach at Thursday Island recalls the island's past.

LEFT: Guns were installed on Thursday Island during World War I as a gesture of defiance against the German raider *Emden,* then roaming the Pacific.

ABOVE: Children coming home from school, Thursday Island.

RIGHT: A Torres Strait Islander prepares strips of turtle meat for sale.

FAR RIGHT, TOP: Cultivated pearls from Torres Strait. The round pearls (top right) are made by inserting a nucleus into the body of the oyster and returning the shell to the sea in a basket. The oyster deposits a layer of nacre (mother-of-pearl) around the nucleus, and the "pearl" is later removed. The blister pearls (below and left) are produced in a similar way, by glueing a half-round nucleus inside the shell.

FAR RIGHT, BOTTOM: Friday Island, Torres Strait. Pearl seeder Sugi Moto implants a nucleus.

OVERLEAF: Murray Islands, Torres Strait. These islands are of comparatively recent volcanic origin. Waier (foreground) clearly shows the rim of a crater, invaded on one side by the sea.

LEFT: The fringing reef in front
of Mer, the largest of the Murray
Islands, Torres Strait, is exposed at
low tide.
BELOW LEFT: The lagoon of Mer Island
is rich in small but edible fish.
BELOW, FAR LEFT: Turtles on Mer
Island. The people of several Torres
Strait islands are being encouraged to
raise green turtles commercially, as the
turtle meat is regarded as a delicacy.
Turtle eggs are removed from nests on
the islands, hatched under supervision,
and the young turtles are fed on fish
and meal to promote rapid growth.
These turtles are about six months
old.
ABOVE: The Murray Islands, which are
of volcanic origin, are covered with
deep soil and carry luxuriant
vegetation.
OVERLEAF: Jardine River, Cape York
Peninsula. Draining a vast area on the
tip of the Peninsula, the Jardine is the
only large Australian river whose
basin remains untouched by any form
of development.

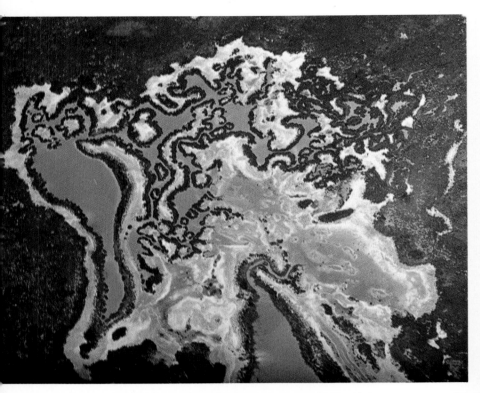

RIGHT: Weipa, Queensland. The red ore of bauxite (aluminium oxide), from which aluminium is smelted, is widely distributed in the tropics. The deposit at Weipa, on the western side of Cape York Peninsula, is one of the richest in the world. The ore, which occurs in a bed many metres thick, is mined by open cut methods and shipped to other centres for smelting.

ABOVE TOP: Water, salt and vegetation have combined to produce these patterns of nature at Weipa — a stark contrast to the imprint of the bauxite mine.

ABOVE: The well preserved wreckage of a fighter aircraft is a reminder of World War II. During the war, hundreds of aircraft operated from airstrips in northern Australia; many aircraft failed to return and are still unaccounted for.

RIGHT: Behind the beach on the western side of Cape York Peninsula there are extensive freshwater lagoons and swamps. This one is near Cape Keer-weer (which means "turn again"). The name was conferred in 1606 by the Dutch navigator Willem Jansz, captain of the *Duyfken*, who was, as far as is known, the first European to reach the coast of Australia. Jansz left the Dutch East Indies to explore the coast of New Guinea, but sailed half-way down the western side of Cape York Peninsula without realising he had discovered the fabled "Great South Land".

ABOVE TOP: Aurukun, south of Weipa, is one of several large missions on the Gulf of Carpentaria.

ABOVE: Estuarine crocodile at Edward River Mission crocodile farm. This is the first project in Australia to raise crocodiles for their skins.

LEFT: Baby crocodiles only a few weeks old have their full array of teeth.

LEFT: Coastline north of Karumba, Queensland. The eastern shores of the Gulf of Carpentaria are so low that a high tide covers the beach and floods the flats (right). Even the mangroves along the beach (left) are temporarily submerged.

BELOW: Along the shallow southern coast of the Gulf of Carpentaria, natural reclamation from the sea is taking place by means of multiple shoreline building. On this section of coast at least four separate shorelines can be seen, where the beach has been successfully colonised by mangroves and other plants, and then extended further seawards and then colonised again.

BOTTOM: On long stretches of the Gulf coastline the only barrier between the ocean (top) and the coastal plain is a dark line of tenacious mangroves.

259

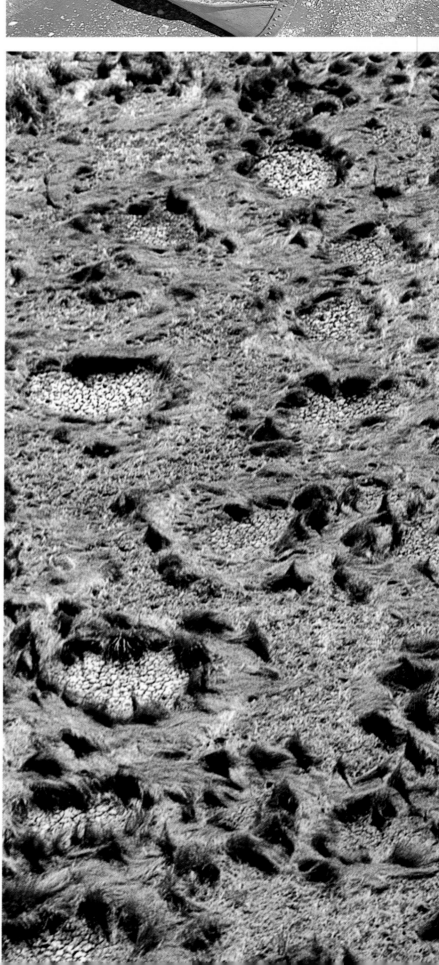

RIGHT: Buffalo wallows on the shores of the Gulf of Carpentaria.

ABOVE: Spring Creek, Gulf of Carpentaria. The meandering of this stream has created an island in the centre of a large loop.

TOP: Barramundi fisherman, Gulf of Carpentaria.

TOP RIGHT: Barramundi fishing in the Smithburn River. These fine eating fish can be netted in almost every river which empties into the Gulf of Carpentaria. The fishermen clean their catch immediately and send it to Karumba, where it is frozen for shipment to southern markets.

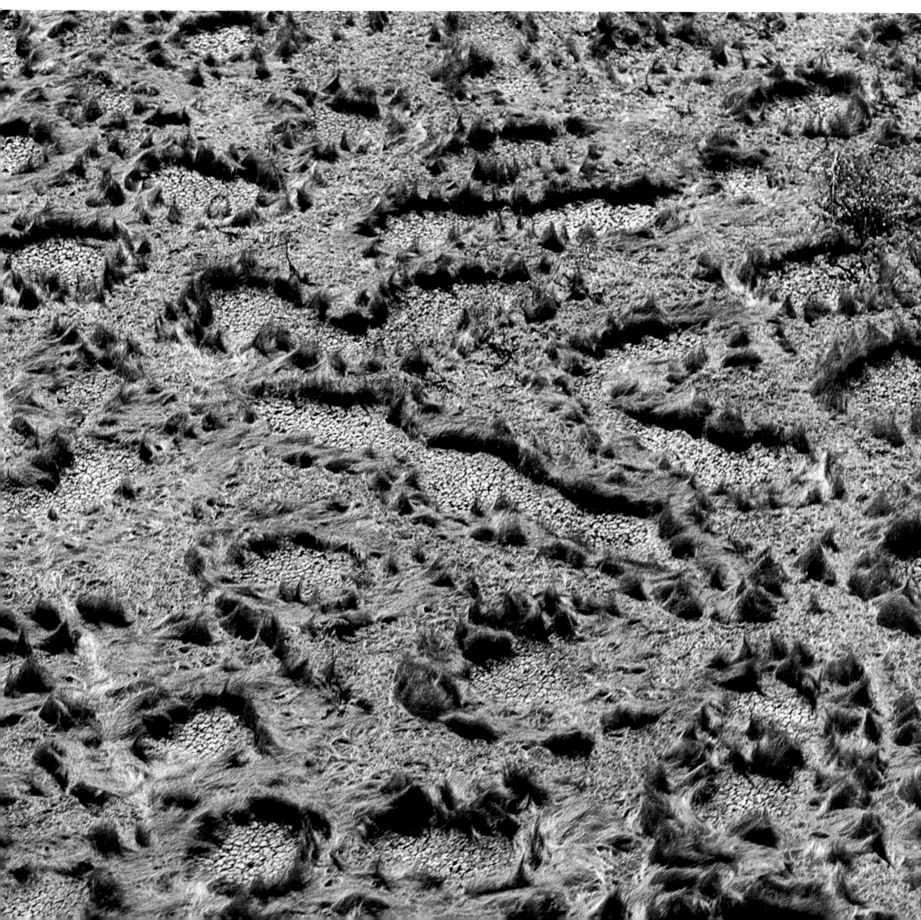

ABOVE: Drainage channels etched in a salt pan near Karumba, Queensland.
RIGHT: Gilbert River, Gulf of Carpentaria. In the wet season the Gilbert is a sluggish flood up to several kilometres wide; in the dry it shrinks to a chain of long pools linked by shallow puddles.
FAR RIGHT: A billabong, filled occasionally by the flooding of Spring Creek, north of Karumba.

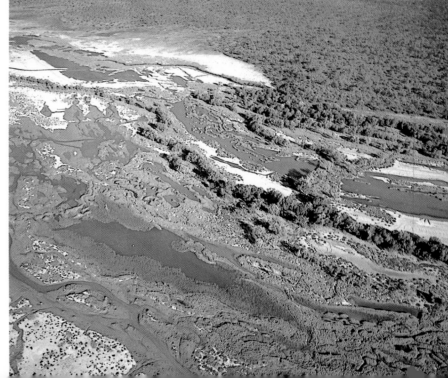

FAR LEFT: Sunrise on the Gulf of Carpentaria.

ABOVE: Loading cattle at Karumba for shipment to the Aboriginal settlement on Mornington Island, in the Gulf of Carpentaria. Karumba is situated near the mouth of the Norman River, and is a port for the cattle stations of the Gulf country.

LEFT: Pelicans on the Norman River at Karumba are not afraid to snatch a fish from an angler's hook.

OVERLEAF: Limmen Bight River, Gulf of Carpentaria. On the southern shore of the Gulf the coastal plain is flatter, the salt flats more extensive and the river meanderings more pronounced than anywhere else on the continent.

ABOVE: Roper River, Northern Territory. Throwing huge loops across the floodplains, the Roper makes a calm and leisurely entrance into the Gulf of Carpentaria, but in its upper reaches it flows through rocky gorges. The river marks the boundary beween the Gulf country and the Arnhem Land plateau, an expanse of ancient fissured rock that includes some of the most inaccessible country in Australia.

RIGHT: Roper River settlement. Originally a mission station, this settlement is now run by the Aboriginal community.

Arnhem Land to Bathurst Island

The great block of Arnhem Land, which forms the western boundary of the Gulf of Carpentaria, and the islands of the Arafura Sea are a fascinating part of the Australian continent. This was almost certainly the major route of entry for the Aboriginal colonisers from Asia. It was also one of the first parts of the coast to be sighted by Europeans. In 1623 the Dutch ships *Pera* and *Arnhem* left Java to explore the west coast of Cape York Peninsula. On their return journey, the crew of the *Arnhem* discovered the north-east coast of a vast new territory, and from that time it has been known as Arnhem Land.

The heart of Arnhem Land is a low, weathered plateau of very ancient rocks, with a steep escarpment on the north-western side. Many large rivers rise in the plateau country, flowing first through the gorges they have cut in the rock, then pouring out across the floodplain towards the marshy coastline. Thick tropical jungles of paperbarks, screw-palms and figs grow along their banks; in the tidal estuaries the mangroves take over.

The tropical north coast, facing the Arafura Sea, is dotted with islands: Croker, Goulburn, Elcho, Melville and Bathurst. Like Arnhem Land itself, these islands have always supported comparatively large Aboriginal populations, and these communities are still flourishing. The people of this part of northern Australia have always had a rich culture, and because of Arnhem Land's remoteness and inaccessibility their culture, beliefs and tribal life have survived the impact of European settlement better than elsewhere in Australia. Conditions are much less suitable for European settlement. There have been a number of attempts to establish ports on the north coast, but Darwin is the only one that has survived.

LEFT: The rocky plateau of Arnhem Land, Northern Territory, has many striking formations produced by erosion, but none more spectacular than the one known as the "Ruined City", north of the mouth of the Roper River. Towers and pinnacles of weathered sandstone, separated by evenly spaced "streets", could from a distance easily be mistaken for the buildings of an abandoned city.

RIGHT: Trial Bay, Northern Territory. This bay, sheltered by a wooded cape (foreground), lies on the western side of the Gulf of Carpentaria. For centuries before European settlement of Australia, the northern coast was visited by the sailing praus of Malay and Macassan fishermen. They would arrive with the north-west monsoon and spend months in the Gulf, collecting bêche-de-mer (trepang). They cooked and dried these marine animals while camping in bays like this, then returned home with the south-east trade winds. From these visitors the Aborigines learned to handle sailing canoes (still used in the north) and obtained steel axes and other tools.

ABOVE: North Point, Groote Eylandt. The Dutch named the largest island in the Gulf of Carpentaria Groote (great) Eylandt. Many low, rocky islets lie off its northern tip.

RIGHT: A bauxite refinery at Gove, Northern Territory. Large deposits of bauxite, the raw material for aluminium, have been found on the Gove Peninsula, at the north-eastern tip of Arnhem Land. The bauxite is treated at Gove to produce alumina powder. The powder is shipped to Gladstone, in Queensland, where it is treated electrolytically and reduced to aluminium ingots.

ABOVE: The overland conveyor belt at Gove which carries the bauxite from the open cut mine to the refinery is one of the longest ever constructed. It extends for 19 kilometres, and the bauxite takes one and a half hours to reach the refinery.

LEFT: Hutchinson Strait, Northern Territory. This apparent river, flanked by mud flats and fed by "tributaries", is in fact a tidal sea channel that separates Howard Island (left) from the mainland at Napier Peninsula. The "river" flows in the direction of the tide.

ABOVE TOP: Gugari Rip, Wessel Islands, Northern Territory. Tides racing through shallow, rocky gaps between islands and reefs make these waters extremely hazardous for shipping.

ABOVE: Marchinbar Island. The rocks on this low island in the Wessel group have weathered along fault lines, producing the effect of giant paving stones.

ABOVE LEFT: Buffaloes on the Liverpool River flood plain. Although called buffaloes, these animals are a type of Indian native cattle introduced into Australia during early attempts to establish settlements on the northern coast. When the settlements were abandoned the surviving buffaloes multiplied and spread across the Northern Territory.

LEFT: Because of their wallowing habits, buffaloes cause severe environmental damage to the swamps and lagoons of the Northern Territory.

ABOVE: A typical tidal estuary on the Arnhem Land coast.

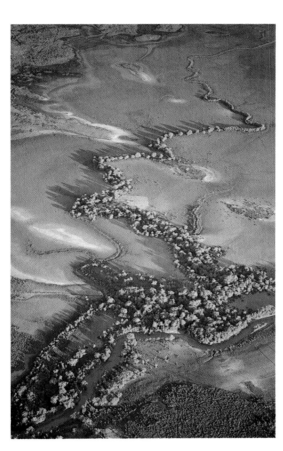

LEFT: East Alligator River plains, Arnhem Land. Between the Arnhem Land escarpment and the Arafura Sea there is a wide, flat coastal plain, covered with grass. The open clay pans may have been caused by grass fires, similar to those on the horizon. Such fires are common in the dry season, and are often started by lightning, or by Aborigines to flush out game.

ABOVE: Evening on the East Alligator River floodplain.

ABOVE RIGHT: Creeks joining the East Alligator River wind across salt pans, their channels marked by mangroves.

RIGHT: Jim Jim Creek, Arnhem Land. Trees mark the course of the creek (foreground) as it emerges from the Arnhem Land escarpment to join other watercourses on the plain. In the dry season such streams are mere trickles; in the "wet" they become torrents.

ABOVE TOP: Arnhem Land escarpment, near Oenpelli. In places the escarpment is a continuous wall, while in others it has craggy outliers rising abruptly from the plain. The huge deposits of the Alligator Rivers uranium province have been found in this area.

ABOVE: Kakadu National Park, Arnhem Land. One of the major national parks in Australia, Kakadu includes a wide cross-section of the magnificent country along the edge of the Arnhem Land escarpment. The lagoons, the home of countless waterbirds and waders, are a characteristic feature of the area.

LEFT: Port Essington, Northern Territory. This tranquil, deserted beach was the scene of an ill-fated attempt in 1838 to establish a trading port on Australia's northern coast. A settlement was built and named Victoria, and port facilities were constructed on a nearby headland. However, the hoped-for trade with South-East Asia failed to develop and in 1849 the "capital city" of northern Australia was abandoned, following similar establishments on Melville Island into oblivion. The effort was not entirely wasted as Victoria had served as a base for much valuable survey work and exploration of the north. Ludwig Leichhardt's historic expedition of 1844-5 ended at Port Essington after a 4800 kilometre journey of extreme hardship from Brisbane.

ABOVE: Ruins at Port Essington. The fireplaces and chimneys of the buildings were carefully constructed of brick. Today they are all that is left standing of the settlement of Victoria.

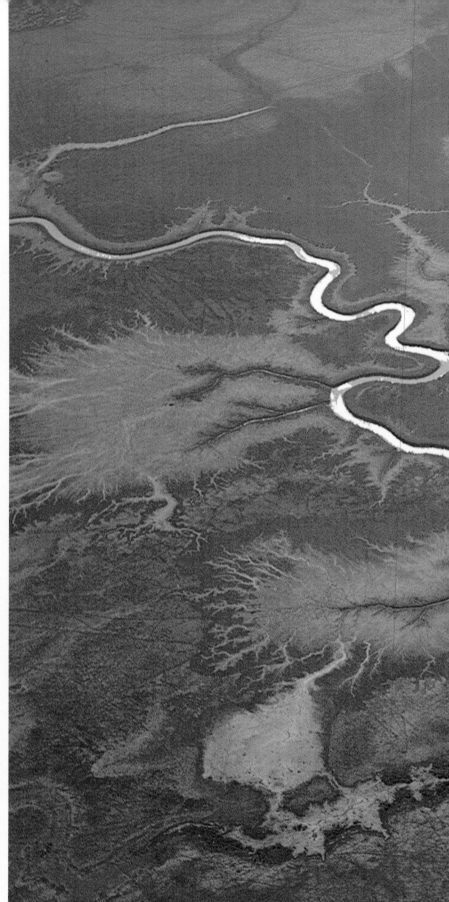

ABOVE: A coastal plain near Darwin, Northern Territory. The coast east of Darwin is a flat expanse of grey mud, across which creeks and rivers run snake-like towards the sea. As the channels become deeper, mangroves establish themselves on the banks.

ABOVE LEFT: Where the streams cross the beach they may form delicate fern-like traceries.

LEFT: In tidal channels the drying salt forms a gleaming white crust.

ABOVE: A Darwin residential area, now rebuilt after almost complete destruction by Cyclone Tracy.

RIGHT: Reserve Bank, Darwin. The city of Darwin is the capital of the Northern Territory, which obtained self-government in July 1978 and became, in effect, Australia's seventh State.

FAR RIGHT: Darwin Harbour, Northern Territory. The only port on the north coast, Darwin has seen more drama than any other harbour in Australia: many ships were sunk here by Japanese bombing during World War II, and boats were again lost during Cyclone Tracy in 1974. The harbour was discovered in 1839 by Lieutenant John Stokes in HMS *Beagle,* and named after the naturalist Charles Darwin, who had earlier made his famous journey of discovery in the *Beagle.*

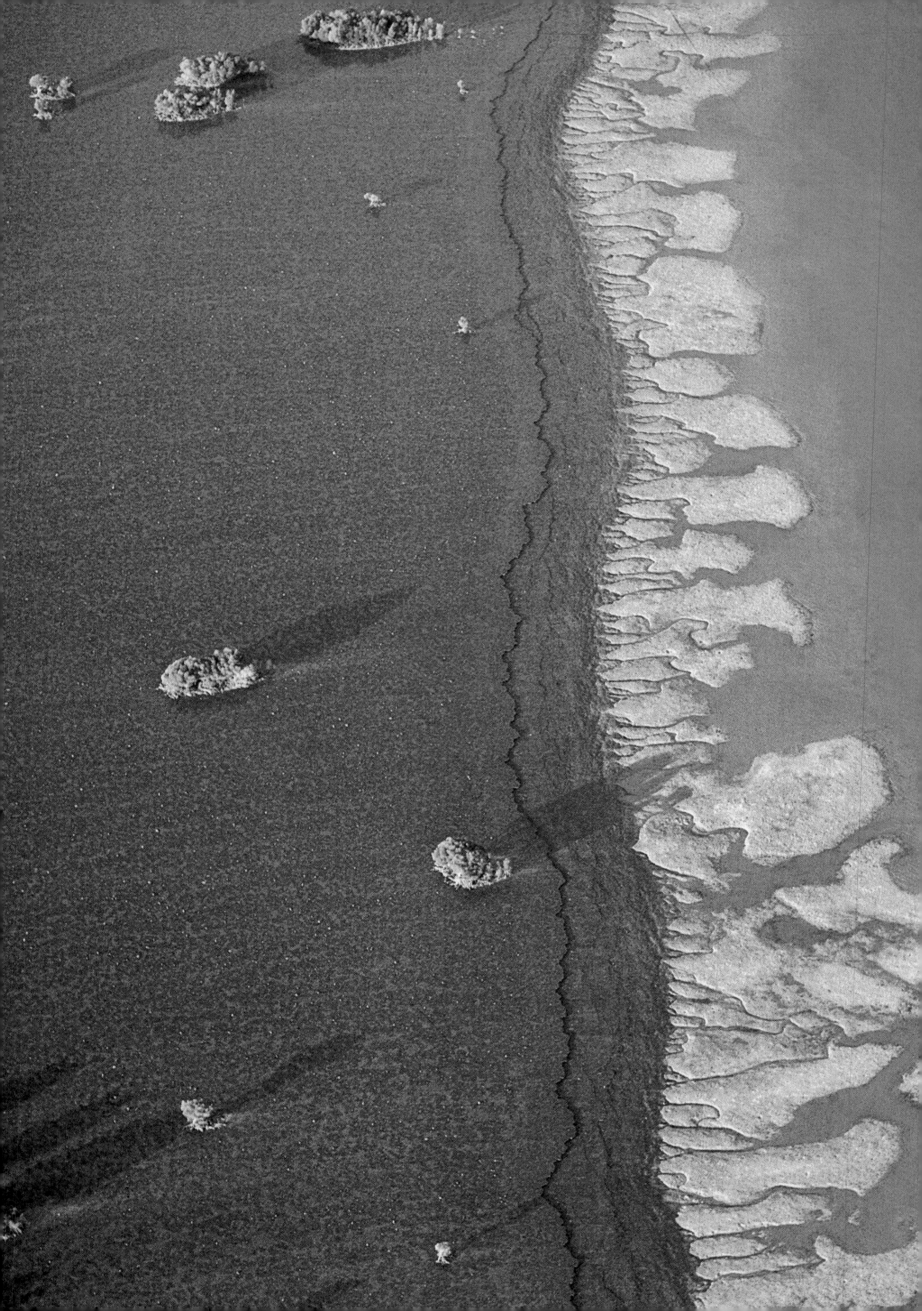

LEFT: Water and sand overlap at the margins of Melville Island, north of Darwin.
ABOVE TOP: Apsley Strait, between Bathurst Island (left) and Melville Island. This was the site of an abortive attempt at European settlement, called Fort Dundas, in 1824. Today both Bathurst and Melville islands have large Aboriginal populations.
ABOVE: Bathurst Island settlement. This former mission station is now run by an Aboriginal council, with help from mission staff.

RIGHT: Bathurst Island craft centre. Many of the artistic skills of the Bathurst Islanders have been adapted to modern technologies. Eddie Puruntatamiri has mastered the potter's wheel, and makes high quality pots and bowls from clay found on the island. The pottery, decorated with traditional designs, is greatly sought after in southern art galleries and craft shops.

ABOVE: An artist in the print shop on Bathurst Island prepares a silk-screen for printing. The centre was set up by European mission workers and has a steady and profitable output of printed wall hangings, dress lengths and other materials.

RIGHT: Rehearsal for funerary rites, Bathurst Island. Traditional life is still very strong in Arnhem Land, particularly on the islands. Here men at the Bathurst Island settlement rehearse a ceremony to mark the first anniversary of the death of a man's wife. The rehearsal takes place behind the houses in the settlement and can be watched by women, children and strangers. The actual ceremony is restricted to men, and will take place in the bush the following night.

ABOVE: The widower paints his body with ceremonial patterns, using paint prepared from natural pigment.

ABOVE LEFT: A dancer raises the dust during the rehearsal.

Victoria River to Derby

Projecting from the north-western coast into the Timor Sea are the Kimberleys, a remarkable geological entity which is quite distinguishable from the rest of the continent. It is in essence a massive plateau of ancient rock. More than 600 million years ago it was an island, separated from the rest of the continent, but the seas have long since retreated from the landward side, and lowlands now extend from the Victoria River in a great arc to the Fitzroy River and the Indian Ocean near Broome.

On the seaward side the edge of the plateau is deeply dissected by the ocean into an extraordinary coastline. Across the centre of the plateau the long processes of erosion have carved gorges and ridges, producing perhaps the most impassable landscape of the entire continent.

The Kimberleys lie in the tropics, and during the wet season a succession of monsoon storms move in from the Indian Ocean and turn the rivers into mighty torrents. It was this abundance of water, and the fertile soils of the river flats, that provided the inspiration for the Ord River Project. However, economic and other problems, such as insect pests, proved insurmountable and the vast water resources of the storage area, Lake Argyle, have never been used for farming.

The deserted coastline of the Kimberleys is cut by narrow, fiord-like gulfs in which tide changes of up to 15 metres take place. Only the isolated islands of Cockatoo and Koolan are populated, being strip-mined for their high-grade iron-ore.

The Kimberleys were named after the fabled diamond fields of South Africa, because of a fancied resemblance seen by an early prospector. Only in 1978 was the early surmise found to have some truth, when diamond-bearing pipes were proved near Derby. For most of their European history the Kimberleys have been best known for their vast beef cattle stations.

LEFT: The interior of the ancient plateau that forms the Kimberleys, in Western Australia, is a landscape of almost unbelievable ruggedness. The surface is eroded and rocky, supporting only the most tenacious trees and clumps of spinifex.

ABOVE: Victoria River, Northern
Territory. The largest river in the
Northern Territory, the Victoria is
about 640 kilometres long. It rises in
the interior and for much of its length
flows through rolling pastoral country,
passing two renowned cattle stations,
Wave Hill and Victoria River Downs.
Near its mouth, however, the river has
cut through a series of ridges
produced by the erosion of tilted folds
in the rocks.

LEFT: Before entering the sea, the
Victoria River spreads to occupy a
broad estuary, which at the river's
mouth is 26 kilometres wide. The river
is tidal for about 160 kilometres and
has been navigated by quite large
ships for at least 80 kilometres.

RIGHT: Ord River Dam, the main dam in the Ord River Scheme, Western Australia. Completed in 1972, it lies in a gorge about 40 kilometres upstream from the town of Kununurra. Lake Argyle, which formed behind the dam, is the largest body of stored water in Australia, but it has never been used for anything other than water sports, fishing and cruising. The water supplied by the original diversion dam near Kununurra has always been sufficient to meet the demands of the few farms that were developed.

ABOVE: The Carr Boyd Range, in the Kimberleys. These tilted folds are typical of the formations in the Kimberleys. They date from pre-Cambrian times, more than 600 million years ago, and are among the oldest exposed rocks in Australia.

OVERLEAF: Lake Argyle. Among the landmarks inundated by the Ord River Dam was the original Argyle Station, established by the pioneering Durack family in 1885. The family completed a tremendous feat of droving thousands of head of cattle overland from Queensland in order to start the station.

LEFT: Trees drowned by the creation of Lake Argyle still stand, bleached by the sun.
ABOVE: Changes in water level from season to season have encouraged new plant growth in the shallow backwaters of Lake Argyle.

LEFT: The small town of Wyndham (background) is located on the estuary of the Pentecost River, Western Australia, where mangrove-lined drainage channels wind across broad salt pans. It began its existence as a port for the Kimberley goldfields, and later became the main meat packing and shipping centre for the Kimberley cattle industry.

BELOW: Safflower at the Kimberley Research Station, Kununurra. When cotton proved difficult to grow economically at Kununurra, safflower was one of the many crops tested for suitability on the irrigated farms of the Ord River Scheme.

RIGHT: Falls on the Mitchell River, in the Kimberleys. Where rivers have cut into the rocky plateau of the Kimberleys spectacular waterfalls occur, even in the dry season. During the monsoon season these falls become thundering cataracts.

ABOVE TOP: Mount Trafalgar in the Kimberleys. Hard cap rock has resisted the erosion which has worn down the surrounding country, to form this remarkable towering mountain.

ABOVE: Kalumburu Mission. In 1908 Benedictine monks from the New Norcia monastery, near Perth, established a lonely mission on the coast of the Kimberleys. The present population is just over 200, nearly all of whom are Aborigines. The mission is renowned for its fruit, vegetables and cattle.

LEFT: Prince Regent River makes its
final approach to the sea through 80
kilometres of an extraordinarily
straight valley, which is in fact a long
fault line in the massive worn-down
plateau of the Kimberleys.

ABOVE: St George Basin, one of several
large inlets on the Kimberley coast
which were formed by a rise in sea-
level about 10,000 years ago. The
Prince Regent River enters this basin
at right angles, beyond the steep cliff
on the right of the picture.

311

RIGHT: Horizontal waterfall, Kimberleys. This unusual spectacle occurs when the tide pours backwards or forwards between the ocean and a large, almost land-locked inlet whose only entrance is this gap, barely 50 metres wide. The tide rises and falls much faster than the water can move through the gap, producing a waterfall, first one way, then the other.

BELOW: Two horizontal waterfalls, produced by narrow gaps which have formed in parallel ridges.

ABOVE: A bay in the McLarty Range, Kimberleys. The fishbone pattern of what appears to be floating vegetation is in fact mangrove trees rooted in mudbanks which are covered by an unusually high tide.

FAR LEFT: Cockatoo Island, Yampi Sound. This island consists almost entirely of high-grade iron ore. The deposit was discovered in 1880, but because of the remoteness of the location, mining did not begin until 1951. The mineworkers and their families live in a township on the island.

LEFT: Koolan Island, Yampi Sound. This deposit, near Cockatoo Island, was opened up in 1965. The ore is shipped direct to Japan.

315

RIGHT: Buccaneer Archipelago, Kimberleys. Tidal races between the islands illustrate the dramatic rise and fall of the tides along this coast.
ABOVE: At the head of King Sound, the largest inlet on the Kimberley coast, the shoreline consists of broad salt-encrusted tidal flats, cut by drainage channels.

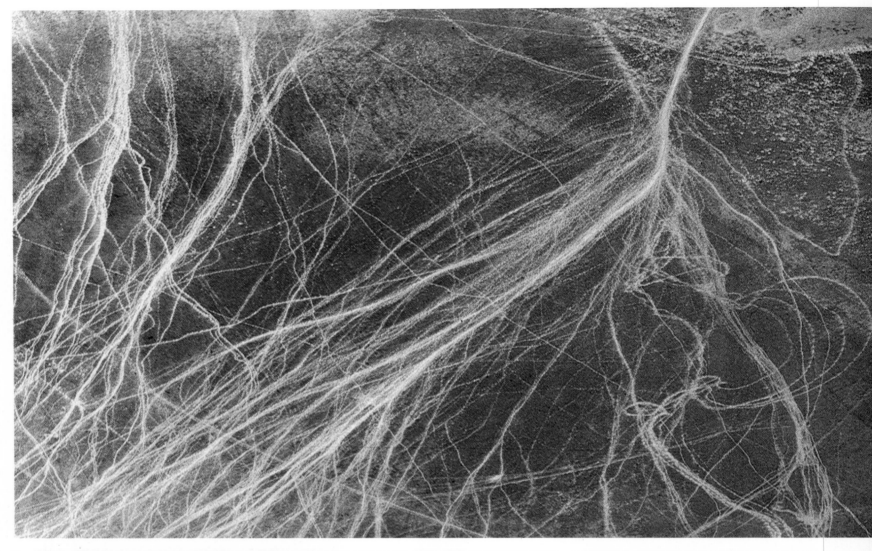

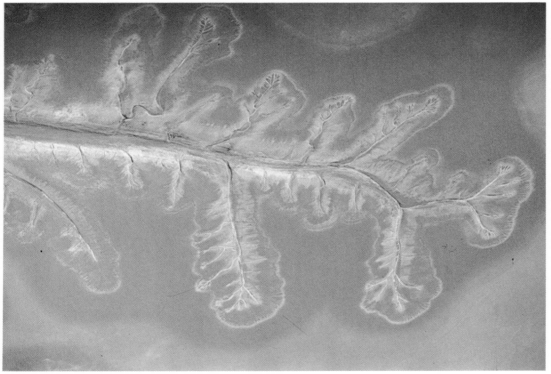

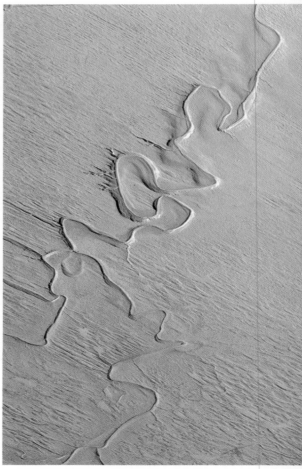

ABOVE: Animal tracks, tides and salt crusts form traceries on the mud flats near Derby, Western Australia. RIGHT: Coastline near Broome, Western Australia. South of King Sound the rocky Kimberley cliffs give way to low banks of red soil and the coastline begins to take on a low profile once again.

Broome to Cape Leeuwin

The long curve of Australia's west coast, from the Kimberleys to Cape Leeuwin, has one striking feature: its uniformity. Along almost its entire length of more than 2000 kilometres there is little change in the sweep of low coastline, washed by rolling swells from the Indian Ocean which crash on white sand beaches or low reefs along the water's edge. There are no mountain ranges within sight of the coast, no deep or steep-walled gulfs, only the broad shallow embayments of Shark Bay and Exmouth Gulf. The main reason for the uniform nature of the coast is the overall flatness of the ancient shield which covers much of Western Australia. One of earth's oldest land surfaces, it slopes almost imperceptibly towards the Indian Ocean, forming a gentle incline that continues out to sea for more than 150 kilometres, to the edge of the continental shelf. The coast itself is unusual in being made of a belt of limestone, in some places narrow and in others extending for a long distance inland. This limestone shelf is low, picturesque and extremely rugged, carved by the sea into caves and grottoes, and eroded by rain. In some stretches it forms cliffs, on others flat offshore islands, such as the Houtman Abrolhos group and Rottnest. This was the coast that the early European ships navigated on their way to the East Indies. With no landmarks, few places to shelter and onshore winds forever blowing across the hidden reefs, it is little wonder that it is littered with wrecks, from the *Tryall* (1622) and the *Batavia* (1629) onwards. There was an aura of mystery and isolation about the west coast that was to persist right through its subsequent history of pearling, whaling and crayfishing, to the present day.

LEFT: Zuytdorp Cliffs, Western Australia. In places the coastal limestone forms cliffs more than 250 metres high, against which the waves crash unceasingly. This stretch is named after the Dutch ship *Zuytdorp*, wrecked here in 1712.

ABOVE: Broome, Western Australia. This town was established in the 1880s to exploit the rich pearl beds nearby. By 1910 it was the pearling centre of the world, with nearly 400 luggers.

RIGHT: Roebuck Bay, Broome. William Dampier anchored his ship HMS *Roebuck* here in 1699 — the first recorded European visit to the area.

CENTRE RIGHT: The cemetery at Broome contains the graves of scores of divers of many races who died in the hunt for pearls.

FAR RIGHT, TOP: Gantheaume Point, Broome, an outcrop of strikingly coloured weathered sandstone.

FAR RIGHT, BOTTOM: Pearlshell, now coming back into fashion for buttons, still brings in a good income for some inhabitants of Broome.

FAR LEFT: The shallowness of the water off Eighty Mile Beach, Western Australia, illustrates the almost imperceptible slope of the coastline south of Broome.

ABOVE TOP: Eighty Mile Beach is an unbroken sweep of sand.

ABOVE AND LEFT: At low tide Eighty Mile Beach becomes even wider as shelving sandbanks are exposed.

ABOVE: Iron ore from the Pilbara is one of Australia's most valuable exports. Most of it goes to Japan in bulk carriers such as this one, at the Dampier loading wharf.

RIGHT: Ore from the Pilbara is carried from the inland mines by rail and stockpiled at the Dampier wharf, ready for loading.

FAR RIGHT: An oil rig off Dampier, Western Australia. A new era is opening up for the west coast, with the development of the oil and gas resources of the North West Shelf. Very large floating drilling rigs such as this are needed to explore the deep waters off the coast.

RIGHT: Saltworks, Dampier. This patchwork of salt ponds is one of the world's major sources of salt. As the seawater is pumped from one pond to another, the hot sun causes more and more evaporation to occur and the concentration of salt steadily increases. In the final pond the salt forms a layer of pure white crystals, which will be harvested by large scrapers. In summer as much as one million tonnes of sea water evaporates from the ponds daily.

ABOVE: The Dampier saltworks has a capacity to produce 3 million tonnes of salt per year.

FAR RIGHT: Yardie Creek, North West Cape, Western Australia. The promontory which forms North West Cape consists of a low wedge of weathered limestone. In places the monsoon rains have cut deep creek beds in the sides of the ridge.

ABOVE TOP: Herds of wild goats thrive on the bushes and scattered grass of the coastal plain near Cape Range.

ABOVE: Shell middens, indicating places where catches of shellfish were regularly eaten, tell the story of a long history of occupation of the west coast by Aborigines.

RIGHT: Aboriginal rock peckings of great antiquity occur in many places on the north-west coast.

LEFT: Cape Inscription, Dirk Hartog Island. In 1616 the Dutch navigator Dirck Hartog landed at the tip of this island, which is located at the entrance to Shark Bay, Western Australia. This was the first recorded European landing on the west coast, and to mark his discovery Hartog nailed an inscribed plate to a post on what is now called Inscription Point. Willem de Vlamingh discovered Hartog's plate in 1696, replaced it with one of his own, and took the original to Amsterdam, where it is still on display. Vlamingh's plate was discovered in 1818 by Louis de Freycinet, who took it to France.

ABOVE: Vlamingh's plate, which was returned from France in 1947, is now in the Fremantle Museum.

OVERLEAF: Salt-making ponds on Lake MacLeod, Western Australia.

RIGHT: Carnarvon, Western Australia. Situated beside the broad sandy lower reaches of the Gascoyne River, Carnarvon is the outlet for a vast district producing wool, cattle and minerals. Tropical fruit and vegetables are grown on irrigated farmland beside the river.

ABOVE: The space-tracking station at Carnarvon. Set up in 1964 by the United States National Aeronautics and Space Administration, it played an important role in the Apollo moon missions by maintaining communication with the astronauts. Today a major satellite communications station is also located at Carnarvon.

FAR LEFT: Murchison River, Western Australia. The most spectacular part of this river course is the Murchison Gorge, which extends for some 80 kilometres through rugged country. This scenic area is now contained within the Kalbarri National Park.

ABOVE TOP: A low plateau backs the south-western coastal plain, its slopes and summit verdant with improved pasture.

ABOVE: A coastal lagoon is dyed a pale mauve by algae and chemicals.

LEFT: Nambung National Park, near Perth. These strange formations of limestone, some as high as 6 metres, stand on a wind-swept stretch of sandhills near the coast. Some geologists believe the pillars were formed underground and then exposed by wind erosion.

FAR RIGHT: Long Island, one of the low limestone islands and reefs making up the Houtman Abrolhos group, off Geraldton. These islands were the scene of one of the most bizarre episodes in Australia's history, the wreck of the *Batavia*. This Dutch ship hit a reef in the group in 1629, and all but 70 of the more than 300 crew and passengers reached the islands. Unable to find water, the captain, Francois Pelsaert, took small boats and most of his crew and sailed to Batavia for help. While he was absent, some of the remaining crewmen mutinied and massacred most of their fellow survivors. When Pelsaert returned, the mutineers were hanged.

ABOVE AND RIGHT: Today the Houtman Abrolhos group is used by fishermen from Geraldton. During the crayfishing season the men live on the islands in small huts built on the limestone, only a metre or so above sea level.

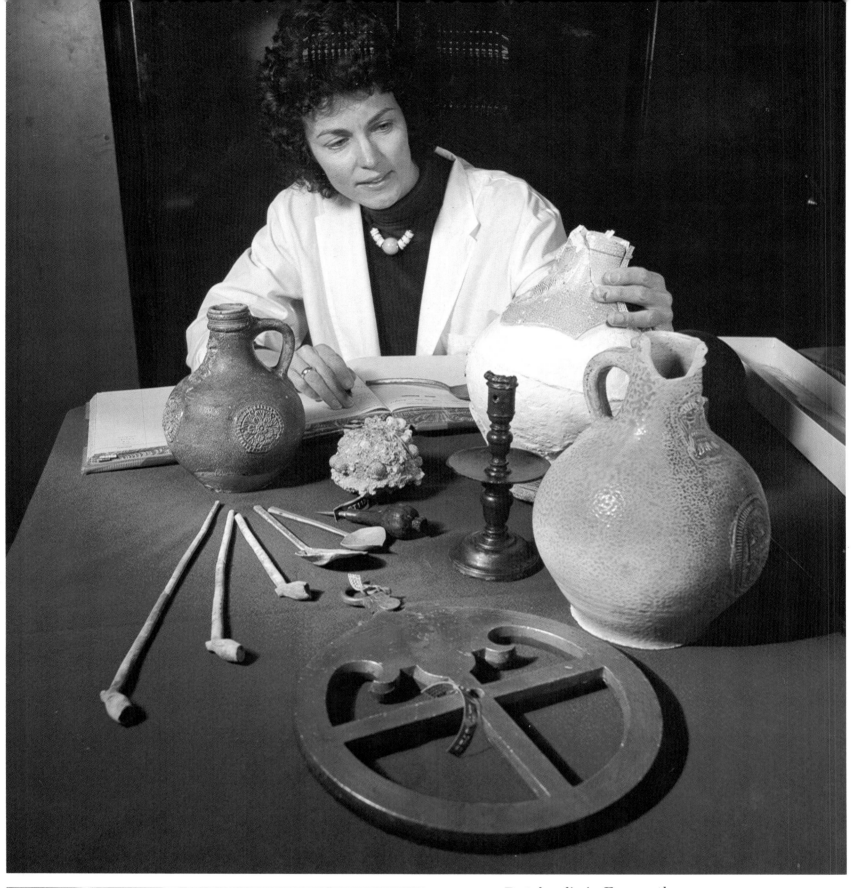

FAR LEFT: Dutch relic in Fremantle Museum, Western Australia. Among the best preserved objects salvaged from the many Dutch wrecks along the west coast are Bellarmine glazed stoneware jugs, some of which have ornate decorations on the neck.

ABOVE: A member of the staff at the Fremantle Museum examines some of the items recovered from Dutch wrecks. The brass instrument (foreground) is an astrolabe, used for navigation.

LEFT: Silverware from the *Batavia*. Although now fragile, some of the pieces have survived well.

OVERLEAF: Perth, the capital city of Western Australia. Located on the banks of the Swan River, Perth was first settled in 1829 and is today the fifth largest city in Australia.

LEFT: Rottnest Island, Western Australia. This low, indented island lying off Fremantle is made of limestone, eroded almost to sea-level. It was named by the Dutch navigator Willem de Vlamingh, who selected the Dutch word for "rat's nest" after finding many small greyish animals scuttling about among the trees. They were in fact quokkas, a species of small wallaby.

BELOW: Rottnest Island is a popular holiday resort for the people of Perth.

RIGHT: Lake Preston, one of several
extensive freshwater lagoons behind
the coastal dunes south of Perth.
ABOVE TOP: Mandurah. This little town
on Peel Inlet, just south of Perth, is
growing steadily as more and more
people in the Perth metropolis look for
somewhere along the coast to live.
ABOVE: Bunbury, a large port south of
Perth, is dominated by a huge
stockpile of eucalypt woodchips
waiting to be shipped to Japan. There
is considerable controversy over
whether or not this is the best use of
timber resources.
OVERLEAF: Cape Leeuwin, Western
Australia. The starting point of
Matthew Flinders' circumnavigation of
Australia — and the end of this
modern voyage of discovery.

Index

Note: Picture references are set in italics.